10 MOST TREASURED
KOREAN CLASSICS

Korean Culture & History Series

10 MOST TREASURED
KOREAN CLASSICS

Publishing Date | July 10, 2010
Published by The KIATS Press, Seoul, Korea
Publishing Director | Jae-Hyun Kim
Narrators | Hyun-Jung Park, Young-Ran Son
Translator | Peter S. Kim
English Editor | Helena R. Chung
Illustrator | Gou Sue
ISBN 978-89-93447-17-0 ISBN 978-89-93447-21-7(set)

10 MOST TREASURED
KOREAN CLASSICS

| Narrated by **Hyun-Jung Park, Young-Ran Son** |
| Translated by **Peter S. Kim** |
| Illustrated by **Gou Sue** |

A Word from the Publisher

In the world, the status of Korea has been elevated high beyond anyone's expectation in recent years. From semiconductors to automobiles to Kimchi, the representative Korean cuisine, the small nation of the Korean Peninsula draws the interest of the world. Along with these developments, the culture and historical legacy of Korea passed down to us by our ancestors have been receiving much attention. Now, it is an urgent necessity to discover, cultivate, and extend the taste, fashion, values, and significance of what is uniquely Korean.

For this reason, we compiled the ten most treasured and widely read Korean classics. The criteria used in selecting only ten out of many classics is as follows: The first criterion asked whether the chosen work can be read by both Koreans in Korea and more than seven million Korean diasporas spread throughout the world. The second asked whether the chosen work appropriately expresses the taste, form, values, and morals as well as the elements of merriment and emotional depth that are the characteristics of Korean classics. The third asked whether the work refrains from overly excessive or technical content in its religious overtones or plot development. In the end, the stories that are entertaining and conventional enough for any Korean to readily read were selected.

This book intends for a relaxed reading such as the story told by one's parents or grandparents. Additional notes attached to the beginning and the end of each story are designed to aid the reader's understanding of the stories. However, if the reader feels these commentaries are difficult to understand or even unnecessary, the stories can be sufficiently read apart from them. You are invited to view the life and culture of our Korean ancestors through this book.

From the very beginning, the publication of this book had English readers in mind and was, thus, produced both in Korean and English. The simultaneous reading in Korean and English will aid learning both languages and their expressions. In this way, Korean readers will become acquainted with English expressions and English readers with Korean expressions.

Many contributed to the process of publishing this book. Hyun-Jung Park and Young-Ran Son helped with the selection and narration of the stories. Hyo-Won Lee carried out the work of editing the manuscript. Peter Kim did the English translation. Helena Chung edited the book into children-friendly words and expressions. Finally, Gou Sue clothed all the stories with the finest illustrations.

2010, *Jae-Hyun Kim*, publisher

CONTENTS

Chun-Hyang Jeon

The Story of Chun-Hyang

The Story of Chun-Hyang is a love story between two persons who were of different social classes. Today, it still remains the most well-known love story of Korean literature which receives the greatest affection. *Love* has been the best material of literature for a long time and it continues to be today.

In the Joseon Dynasty, the caste system was so strict that it was not allowed or even imagined to marry someone from a lower class. Wol-Mae, the mother of Chun-Hyang, was a *gisaeng* ^{mistress} taken by the judiciary court and belonged to a very low social class. Wol-Mae met a man of the *yangban* class ^{high class} and later gave birth to Chun-Hyang. However, because her mother belonged to a low social class, Chun-Hyang was not accepted in the *yangban* class. By chance, Chun-Hyang met a man of the *yangban* class named Yi Mong-Ryong, whom she fell deeply in love with. Being from different social classes and threatened by society, it was difficult for them to keep their love.

The Story of Chun-Hyang is indeed a story of a woman of courage and wisdom that willed herself to keep an impossible love, thereby ultimately achieving her happiness. Chun-Hyang was a daring and passionate woman who went as far as bravely holding onto a man who was leaving her behind for Seoul. Chun-Hyang kept the faith of her love until the end without giving in the threat and pressure of Magistrate Byeon.

The Story of Chun-Hyang has been passed down from generation to generation as an oral tradition with an anonymous author. So, when did *The Story of Chun-Hyang* get its start? It is said that the character of Chun-Hyang is based on a real person. In Namwon, in which *The Story of Chun-Hyang* is set, there was a daughter of an old *gisaeng*. Unlike the novel, however, the daughter was not a beautiful woman, and she was believed to have died without satisfying her unreturned love. So, *The Story of Chun-Hyang* was written and dedicated to this poor woman so that her soul would feel comforted.

Now, shall we see how Chun-Hyang's love comes to bloom?

During the rule of King Sukjong (1661–1720) of Joseon, there was a famous *gisaeng* named Wol-Mae in Namwon, Jeolla Province. Wol-Mae, having retired from her position as a *gisaeng*, spent her remaining days with a gentleman named Mr. Seong, but was always lonely since she did not have any children. So everyday she cleansed herself, traveled to every well-known mountain and prayed with absolute sincerity for a child. Had Wol-Mae's prayer reached the heavens? One day, after having dreamt a mysterious dream of a fairy coming down on a crane, she became pregnant.

When the labor pains started after ten months, a slight fragrance and a five-colored cloud spread in the room, and a baby as beautiful as jade was born. Wol-Mae was as happy as gaining the whole world. She named the baby Chun-Hyang, which meant 'spring fragrance,' and raised her as if she would treat gold and jade.

Time went by, and Chun-Hyang grew up to be a beautiful 16-year-old girl. She always had books near her and, not only were her manners excellent, but she had the deepest and highest respect towards her mother. Everyone would compliment her.

It was during the *Dano* festival in May. *Dano* is one of Korea's traditional holidays, and is celebrated on the fifth day of the fifth month of the lunar calendar. On that day, women wash their hair with water infused with irises and play on the swing, while the men wrestle. Chun-Hyang was playing on the swing at a place in Namwon, with a servant girl named Hyang-Dan. As the swing was pushed underneath her and with her legs tumbling from above, her beautiful appearance highlighted by the silhouette of her red skirt invited the involuntary gaze of others.

Indeed, there was a young man named Yi Mong-Ryong, the son of a government official in Namwon, who was glancing at Chun-Hyang as she played on the swing. Sixteen years of age,

Mong-Ryong was fine in appearance, excelled in academics, and was a specialist of arts—indeed, the noble of nobles. On this day, Mong-Ryong had come out to catch a breathe of spring air, for he was tired of reading books.

"Bangja, what are those waves of colors, going this way and that, in the forest over there?"

After a careful look towards the forest, Bangja answered, "Are you speaking of Chun-Hyang, the daughter of the *gisaeng* Wol-Mae?"

"Oh my, a daughter of a *gisaeng*? Good. I am bored and I could use a conversation partner. Go and bring her here."

"Oh no sir, my young master. You cannot be serious! Her mother may be a *gisaeng* but her father was a government official, and the child was brought up as precious and upright as any girl from a *yangban* family."

"Well, your words just make me curious all the more. I would very much like to meet her. Go and ask her politely."

After a considerable effort on the part of Bangja in going back and forth repeatedly, Chun-Hyang and Mong-Ryong were finally able to meet.

Mong-Ryong became enchanted by Chun-Hyang's angelic face and the way she was standing with a certain feeling of shyness. Chun-Hyang blushed red when she saw that the boy had a beautiful face expression and brilliant eyes.

"I hear that we are both sixteen years of age, and that you are also a precious only child and daughter of your family. Well, it is the fate of heaven that has brought us together. How about you and I get to know each other?"

In this way, Mong-Ryong confessed his love driven by his youthful passion. Chun-Hyang, however, shook her head and replied, "You are a son belonging to a respectable family, but I am only a daughter of a lowly *gisaeng*. If you abandon me after giving me your affections, I would have to spend the rest of my life in tears. I do not wish to do that."

"I swear that I will never abandon you no matter what happens. How could a man of his word say two different things from one mouth? Wait for me and I will come and visit you at your house tonight."

Then, Mong-Ryong returned home, opened up his books again and tried to read. But he could not focus because Chun-Hyang's face continued to captivate his thoughts. He waited until sunset and went over to Chun-Hyang's house.

Wol-Mae, the mother of Chun-Hyang, was really surprised to see that Mong-Ryong had suddenly come to see her daughter. "I saw in my dream that Chun-Hyang went up to the heavens riding on a dragon's back. Now I see that the dream was foreshadowing Chun-Hyang's relationship with Mong-Ryong 夢龍, dragon in dream."

14

Greatly rejoicing, Wol-Mae approved of Chun-Hyang and Mong-Ryong's relationship. Finally, the two vowed and toasted to their love.

Come here—let me carry you
Dear love, love, love—my love
Hey, ho, you are my love

Away from Mong-Ryong's father, Chun-Hyang and Mong-Ryong met every day. The laughter of the two lovers never seemed to end.

Then one day, Mong-Ryong came into Chun-Hyang's house with an expression of despair. He did nothing but sigh.

When Chun-Hyang asked him what was wrong, Mong-Ryong answered,

"Chun-Hyang, what am I to do? My father has been promoted to be an official for the central branch. We must leave for Hanyang ^{Seoul} soon."

"Why, your father has been promoted, and all you can do is cry? You should be rejoicing!"

"Well... I really don't know! I have to leave you here and it's breaking my heart! That's why I'm crying."

Chun-Hyang was completely surprised to hear this. Drawing closer to Mong-Ryong, she asked,

"My Lord, what are you saying? You can't take me with you? Did you not give me the matrimonial cup and promise that you would never abandon me, no matter what happened? Do you dare to abandon me just because I am a daughter of a lowly *gisaeng*?"

"Chun-Hyang, that could never be! My father would surely give me hell if I told him now. It's just that I cannot tell him about us right now."

"Well, then what am I to do? I'll be all alone here. No, no. I cannot let that happen!"

"Chun-Hyang, am I leaving you for good? How could I forget you even if I moved to Hanyang? I shall study hard and pass the exam and come back to take you with me. I promise."

Chun-Hyang held onto the edge of Mong-Ryong's trousers and cried desperately. Mong-Ryong cried with her as he tried to comfort her. In this way, they spent their last night together and Mong-Ryong left for Hanyang in the morning.

A whole year went by since Mong-Ryong had left for Hanyang.

But without any news from Mong-Ryong, Chun-Hyang became weary of waiting and got ill.

Meanwhile, a new district magistrate for the region of Namwon was chosen. His name was Byeon Hak-Do. Hak-Do, very much partial to drinks and women, searched for a *gisaeng* as soon as he was appointed.

"I hear the *gisaeng*s of these parts are the best in the country. Am I right?"

"Yes, sir."

"I also hear that the girl named Chun-Hyang is the prettiest of them all."

His deputy answered, "Magistrate, the mother of Chun-Hyang was a *gisaeng*, but Chun-Hyang is not. And... I am very sorry to tell you this, but Chun-Hyang is already engaged to the son of the former magistrate of this town. She is only waiting for him to return and take her with him."

"You fool! Do you know who the former magistrate is? How could his son ever enter into relationship with such a lowly girl? If you value your own life, you will stop giving excuses and bring Chun-Hyang to me."

The deputy could no longer put him off. He went to Chun-Hyang, and begged, "Chun-Hyang, no one doubts your faithfulness.

I know it, you know it, and heaven knows it. But we, lowly
servants, will be killed because of you. There is no other way.
Let us rush and go to the magistrate."

When Chun-Hyang walked into the front yard of the regional
court, Hak-Do slapped his knees, extremely impressed by her
beauty.

"The prettiest of them all indeed! Chun-Hyang, you shall serve
me starting this very night."

However, Chun-Hyang held her head up high, and answered,

"Magistrate, certainly, I am thankful beyond I can say, but
I am already engaged to another man. I cannot fulfill your
request."

Hak-Do sneered in a loud laughter and then tried to convince
her by saying,

"Look at this girl of firm loyalty! However, how could such a
highly regarded family such as that of Magistrate Yi ever receive
someone like you as his daughter-in-law? And do you think his
son would remember you, a girl he'd merely played with in his
immature days of youth? Don't waste your precious youth and
regret when you are older. Listen to me."

"A servant could never serve two kings; I could never have two husbands. Let it end at that."

"You're an ignorant girl, who has no ability to listen! Listen carefully! Not a word of what I'm telling you is getting through to you, is it? Listen! Those who do not follow the commands of the magistrate, I will punish with the harshest of the sentences. Don't blame me even if you die!"

"Really? Well, what kind of punishment is there for a man who wants to rape a woman already married?"

"Shut up! You wretch! Hey, beat her, and tie her up to the *juri*!"

Juri was a type of torture in which a person's legs are tied together, and two sticks are inserted and twisted between them. Chun-Hyang was beaten to a pulp and was sent to jail.

Meanwhile, Yi Mong-Ryong, who had left to Hanyang, was able to earn the top place among those who passed the government entrance exam. He was soon appointed as a secret commissioner for the king.

In order to secretly determine the reputations of regional officials, Mong-Ryong disguised himself in a ragged coat and *gat* ^{a traditional hat} and set foot into Namwon.

As Mong-Ryong sat on a hill to catch his breath, he saw a young man rushing up the hill. When he looked at him closely, he saw that it was Bangja who was once his servant.

Pushing his *gat* deep down, Mong-Ryong asked, "Hey there! Where are you going in such a hurry?"

"I'm taking Chun-Hyang's letter to Yi's residence in Hanyang."

"Really? Well, let me see that letter."

"Why would you want to read a married woman's letter?"

"Huh, huh, well, I want to read it all the more because it is a married woman's letter! What do you think?"

As he argued over the letter with Mong-Ryong, Bangja suddenly stood up straight in shock. He realized that the face and voice of the man was awfully familiar.

Only then, Mong-Ryong revealed his face, saying, "Bangja, can't you recognize me?"

"Oh, my lord! Why have you come so late? Chun-Hyang is half dead from being beaten by the magistrate. I was taking what may be Chun-Hyang's last letter to Hanyang, to find you."

Bangja bowed down before Mong-Ryong and then handed him the letter.

Since we bade farewell, you have not written me. I am worried that my lord may not be well. I refused the new magistrate's command to become his mistress, and for that

I have been imprisoned. I now wait only for the day of my death. I am not afraid of dying, but my heart breaks at the thought of my mother being on her own... My lord, it is my last wish to see your face one more time before I die.

Sometime last year, I bade thee farewell—
A couple of days ago, it snowed
and now the leaves fall once again.
My tears fall down in this deep, dark, wintry night—
Me, a prisoner in jail—could this be? Is this a dream?

Having read Chun-Hyang's letter, Mong-Ryong was able to grasp her situation. Speeding up his steps, he walked all night and arrived at Chun-Hyang's house, to find her mother Wol-Mae praying with a bowl of water in the corner of the front yard.

"I beg, I beg, I beg to the gods of heaven and earth. My precious Chun-Hyang has been beaten and imprisoned when she is innocent. Please, let Yi Mong-Ryong, who has gone to Hanyang, pass his exam and hurry back here to save the life of my daughter."

As he listened to the sound of the prayer, he became emotional thinking that it was to his mother-in-law's credit that he passed the exam. As he opened the gate of the house and entered, he shouted in a confident voice, "Mother-in-law, I am here. Your son-in-law has come back from Hanyang!"

"Oh my, oh my, what a coincidence is this? Why have you come so late? Were you brought here by the wind? Surrounded by a blanket of cloud? You received the news about Chun-Hyang and came to save her!"

Wol-Mae was grateful beyond words at first. However, upon a second look, and under better light, she was now speechless for a different reason. She had thought Chun-Hyang would be released from prison upon her son-in-law's arrival, but Mong-Ryong was in the appearance of a beggar. She thought, 'Now, my Chun-Hyang is certainly going to die.'

Not aware of Wol-Mae's feelings, Mong-Ryong continued to push her to take him to Chun-Hyang.

"Chun-Hyang!"

When Wol-Mae called her daughter, who had been dozing off with the *kal* A *kal* is a restraint forced on prisoners. It is a long, wide piece of wood with a hole at the end, which is fitted around the prisoner's neck so that it is nearly impossible to move.

around her neck, Chun-Hyang opened her eyes.

"Chun-Hyang, he is here!"

"Who? Who is here?"

"A beggar. I mean, your husband."

When Chun-Hyang saw that the man near Wol-Mae was Mong-Ryong, the one she had been dreaming of coming, she rejoiced greatly. However, when she saw what he was wearing, she could not help but shed a few tears. She asked Hyang-Dan to sell some of her ornaments and clothes, and with the money, get Mong-Ryong some new clothes.

"My lord, tomorrow is the magistrate's birthday. When he gets drunk, he will call upon me and torture me once again. Should I die? My lord, please take my body and bury it in a place that receives much sunlight."

Mong-Ryong answered,

"Do not cry, Chun-Hyang. Isn't there a saying, 'Even if the sky collapses, there bounds to be a hole out of which you can break free.'"

In the face of Mong-Ryong's carefree attitude, Chun-Hyang could not help but mourn her current status.

The next day, governors of other towns, government officials, magistrates, and *yangbans* came to celebrate Byeon Hak-Do's birthday. Colorful tents were installed, and musical performances and the dances of *gisaengs* continued.

When the party reached its peak, a beggar came in with a brave strut. It was, of course, Mong-Ryong. "I am a beggar who happened to be walking by. It seems like an enjoyable party. Bring out a table of food for me, too."

Byeon Hak-Do was not thrilled with the idea, but not wanting to spoil the party, he ordered that a table be brought out for him. As a payment for the food, he ordered Mong-Ryong to compose him a poem. Mong-Ryong emptied a cup of alcohol into his mouth and picked up a writing brush.

The fragrant drink in the bronze cup is the blood of the people,
And the fatty meat on the plate made of jade
is the fat of the people.
When the wax of the candle falls,
so do the tears of the people,
And where there is loud singing,
the people grumble even louder.

Mong-Ryong wrote the poem in a flash, and without addressing the magistrate, he disappeared like the wind. Some of the guests,

who were able to read Mong-Ryong's writing were very much stunned. Realizing that it was a secret commissioner of the king who had written this poem, they quietly left the party. However, Magistrate Byeon and the rest of the guests, who were as drunk as they could possibly get, were busy with the *gisaeng*s and paid no attention to the poem.

The drunk magistrate now asked Chun-Hyang, who was dragged out of jail, to be brought to him. "Will you still refuse me, you wretch?" he asked.

"I'd rather you kill me instead."

Seeing Chun-Hyang's firm posture, the magistrate became even angrier. He screamed, "You, over there! Beat her!"

It was at that very moment, a voice was heard,

"Here is the secret commissioner for the king!"

Soldiers holding six-sided clubs came out of nowhere. The party soon became a scene of chaos. Food was tossed in all directions, and the *gisaeng*s and the musicians ran away. The drunken guests scattered all over the place leaving behind their

hats and linen socks. The magistrate, who also tried to disappear with the crowd, was captured by one of the soldiers and was brought before the commissioner.

"Byeon Hak-Do, the deputy delegate of Namwon, you have harassed innocent people and wasted the tax of the people for your personal use. I therefore take over all your possessions and strip you of your title!"

After Magistrate Byeon and his servers were dragged out, Mong-Ryong called out the prisoners, one by one, inquired of their crimes, and set free the ones who were innocent.

It was finally Chun-Hyang's turn. Mong-Ryong, covering his face with his fan, asked Chun-Hyang,

"What is your name?"

"I am called Chun-Hyang."

"For what sin have you been imprisoned?"

"I refused the magistrate's order to become his mistress. For that, I was imprisoned."

"A *gisaeng*'s daughter dared to refuse a deputy's order to keep her own faithfulness? You deserve to die for that, but if you would be *my* mistress, I shall let you live. Will you do so?"

"Ha, every deputy or magistrate that comes down here is indeed a great one. I see. Listen, secret commissioner. Does a rock on a high cliff fall just because the wind blows, and does a green tree change just because it snows? Stop this nonsense and just kill me."

The commissioner, who was listening to Chun-Hyang's words carefully, came down to the yard where she was, and sat before her. Reaching out to hold her hand, he said, "Chun-Hyang, lift your head."

When Chun-Hyang lifted her head, gone was the beggar that she saw around dawn, and Commissioner Mong-Ryong was smiling at her brightly.

"My lord!"

"Yes, it is I!"

The two hugged each other tightly and rejoiced their reunion.

A few days later, Mong-Ryong, having completed his duties, took Chun-Hyang, her mother, and Hyang-Dan to Hanyang. The people of Namwon all came out to bid Chun-Hyang farewell and happiness.

What was the judiciary court like during the Joseon Dynasty?

The judiciary court was a government building where all government affairs took place. The court was divided into *dong-heon*, *gaek-sa*, *hyang-cheong*, and *ok-sa*. *Dong-heon* was the office of the magistrate, the caretaker of the judiciary court. *Gaek-sa*, which hosted the wooden title-plate of the king, was also a guest house for the central government representatives. Court officials that assisted the magistrate worked at *hyang-cheong*. *Ok-sa* was a jail for criminals.

The town magistrate collected taxes and performed other administrative functions and also presided over trials, sentencing and enforcing penal codes. However, administrative affairs were mostly done by court officials. The magistrate, being an outsider and the one nominated by the central government, needed the help from court officials and their knowledge of the local culture and situations. Court officials were divided into *yi-bang* responsible for human resources , *gong-bang* responsible for weights and measures, roads, and bridges , *byung-bang* responsible for military affairs , *yae-bang* responsible for official documents, ceremonies, banquets, and schools , *hyung-bang* responsible for trials and servants , and *ho-bang* responsible for finance, tax, tributes, and family registry. Those court officials were standing on both sides of the criminal during a trial as represented in the picture.

Municipal court of the Joseon Dynast

Sim Cheong Jeon
The Story of Sim Cheong

If *The Story of Chun-Hyang* is a story of love, *The Story of Sim Cheong* is a story about devotion to one's parents. For the people of Korea, it is an important tradition for children to care for their parents in a respectful manner.

The Story of Sim Cheong is a tale of a devoted daughter named Sim Cheong, who gave herself as a sacrificial offering to the sea in order to enable her blind father to gain his sight.

The context of the story is set in the times of the Goryeo Dynasty in the province of Hwangju. However, people of Baengnyeong Island in the western sea and Gokseong County, South Jeolla Province, also claim that the story is set in their towns as well.

The Story of Sim Cheong is a novel by an unknown author told in the form of *Pansori* a traditional Korean narrative song. There is indeed a root legend that provides the material for the beginning of the story. It is a legend that has been handed down at Gwaneum-sa, a Buddhist temple in Gokseong County, South Jeolla Province, that speaks of a virgin named Hong-Jang who was sold as a slave to China for her blind father. The plot that her father gained his sight once she dedicated a Buddhist statue by selling her body is very similar to that of *The Story of Sim Cheong*.

Just as there was the antagonist Byeon Hak-Do in *The Story of Chun-Hyang* who mistreated the main character Chun-Hyang, there is a character named Ppaengdeuk Uhmum in *The Story of Sim Cheong,* who interferes with the kindness of Sim Cheong. But there is no need to worry. As if heaven was amazed by the great devotion of Sim Cheong, she meets a happy ending, whereas Ppaengdeuk Uhmum meets an unfortunate one. Likewise, the principle of promoting goodness and discouraging evil as illustrated in this story line shows that good people become blessed and wicked people get punished. This principle has ultimately been part of our ancestors' deep rooted values.

Now, shall we follow the adventure of the poor but goodhearted Sim Cheong?

Once upon a time, a blind man named Sim Hak-Gyu lived in a town called Dohwa in the province of Hwangju. People called him Sim-bongsa "Sim-the blinded". Since he could not see, Sim-bongsa was unable to read books or work. Because of this, he was supported by his wife who earned money and put food on the table by working as a maid for other people. His wife, Lady Gwak, worked wherever there was a banquet during the day and sewed in the evening.

Though they were poor, the couple's hearts overflowed with love. If there was one thing they lacked, it was that they were childless. They prayed to heaven daily for a child of their own and it did not matter whether the child was a boy or a girl.

One day, in Lady Gwak's dream, a heavenly fairy appeared and bowed to her.

"I am the daughter of the chief fairy in the kingdom of heaven. I committed a serious mistake and I am being banished to the world of humans. Please accept me."

Then the fairy turned into a bright beam of light and entered the body of Lady Gwak.

Ten months later, Lady Gwak gave birth to a daughter that was as pretty as an angel. Sim-bongsa named her Cheong and showered his affection on her as he would cherish gold or jade. However, the happiness was short-lived. After one week of giving birth, Lady Gwak passed away from the world.

Sim-bongsa mourned her death greatly. "My dear, I should have died and you should have lived. How could you leave me behind? How can I, being blind, raise this child alone?"

Sim-bongsa pitied his wife who endured so much suffering only to die in vain. Being blind and a widower, he felt miserable about how to live on. More than anything, he felt sorry for the baby that lost her mother within just a few days of her birth.

"How in the world will I raise her...?"

With the crying baby on his back, Sim-bongsa came to the well where the women of the village were gathered.

"Ladies, I am so sorry. But would you breastfeed this poor, crying baby of mine just this once? Just a little bit of milk in your bodies that is left over from feeding your own children."

From that day on, the women of the village took turns breastfeeding Cheong.

Thanks to the caring Sim-bongsa and help from the village women, the child kept growing without the care of her mother. Reaching seven years of age, she would go around begging for food on behalf of her father at times.

"Being alive, I just make my little one suffer." Sim-bongsa felt sorry for his daughter.

Holding her father's hand tightly, Sim Cheong said,

"Father, do not say such a thing. Since you have raised me until now, I am going to support you from now on."

When she turned fourteen or fifteen, she began working as a maid and was able to make a living with the money and other forms of payment she earned.

"Cheong is truly a good child. Even in her young age, she earnestly supports her father by working as a maid. Moreover, instead of showing that she's burdened, she always has a smile on her face."

In this way, her reputation began to reach even the neighboring villages.

One day, the matriarch of a rich family in a neighboring village invited Cheong over to her house.

"I heard so much about you, Cheong. I have two sons that are all grown up and working as officials in Hanyang. I really want to adopt you as my daughter. Cheong, what do you think about that?"

After bowing respectfully, Cheong said,

"I feel grateful that you think so highly of me. However, if I become your adopted daughter, then who would look after my father? I do appreciate your words, but I just want to serve my father who is solely dependent on me until the day he dies."

The lady nodded and said,

"I only thought of myself. Cheong, you are indeed a faithful daughter. If you cannot be my adopted daughter, then I ask you to visit me often and be my conversation partner."

Then, the lady packed a variety of gifts and food for her.

While Cheong went to the neighboring village and did not return home as the night set, Sim-bongsa became greatly worried.

He could not wait any longer and came out of the house with a staff in his hand. Having reached a stream, he tried to cross the bridge using his staff to find his way, but he ended up falling into the water.

"Help me! Is there anyone around? Please, save me!"

At once, a Buddhist monk who happened to be passing by that moment came to rescue Sim-bongsa and saved him.

After regaining his senses, Sim-bongsa inquired,

"Who is it that saved me?"

"I am a monk from Temple Mongeun-sa."

He was a monk on a fundraising mission. He was going around door-to-door saying blessings for people and receiving donations that people offered to Buddha.

"Now that you have saved a dying man, I do not know how to repay this grace." Out of his grateful heart, he shared and grieved his fate of having to depend on his young daughter.

In response, the monk mumbled something silently to himself out of his pity for him,

"Tut, tut, only if you can give three hundred sacks of rice to Buddha and pray sincerely, then you could open your eyes."

"Hey Mister, what did you just say now? Did you say that I can gain sight if I offer three hundred sacks of rice in devotion?"

"But, your situation seems to me…"

Without thinking it through, Sim-bongsa pledged to give the rice as an offering.

The monk took out a writing brush and paper and wrote, "Sim Hak-Gyu of Dohwa Village, Offering of 300 sacks of rice." 300 sacks of rice was an enormous amount which amounts to about 36 tons.

Only after the monk had left, Sim-bongsa began to worry.

"Oh my, I must be crazy. How could it ever be possible for our situation to give an offering of three hundred sacks of rice? I must not have been in my right mind."

After coming home, Cheong saw a grim look on her father's face and knew that something was wrong. "Father, are you sick? How come you don't look so well?"

"Cheong, don't even call me father. I am an unworthy father."

"Please tell me what is going on."

Sim-bongsa told her about what happened with the monk.

Then, Cheong began to comfort him saying, "If only you can open your eyes, an offering of three hundred sacks of rice is near nothing."

"My dear, it cannot be. Even a bowl of rice is precious to us. In our situation, three hundred sacks of rice are unthinkable."

"Don't worry too much. Let me work on it."

From that day on, Sim Cheong set a bowl of clean water before her and began praying intently. "I pray and pray to Buddha. Please bring sight to my poor father's eyes." If it meant three hundred sacks of rice, she was ready to give even her life.

Then one day, it happened.

The village women were gathered around the well and talking about something.

"Oh my, it is so awful. I heard that people from the ship are going around shopping for a virgin girl."

"I can understand their business is important. But how can they throw a person into the sea alive?"

"That's what I am saying. They say that money is not the problem but it has to be a fifteen-year-old virgin."

Cheong's ears perked up upon hearing these words. Secretly, she went to the people of the ship and inquired.

"I heard that you are shopping for a fifteen-year-old virgin. Is that true?"

"That is correct. We are merchants that travel to faraway places for business. However, the waves here in the sea of Indangsu are untrustworthy and shipwrecks happen from time to time. For that reason, we are trying to calm the sea by offering a sacrifice of a virgin."

Cheong thought that it was an opportunity given to her by heaven.

"I am fifteen years old. Buy me."

Cheong told them about her situation. She said she would agree to be the sacrifice if they would send three hundred sacks of rice to Temple Mongeun-sa. The people of the ship were so touched by Cheong's filial piety that they agreed to pay enough money for Sim-bongsa to live comfortably in addition to the three hundred sacks of rice.

Time passed and the promised day came. Swallowing tears, Cheong cooked warm rice. She sat right across from her father and put meat pieces on his spoon.

"Father, eat to your heart's content."

"Yes, but I must say that today's side dishes are unusually great. Was there a banquet somewhere?"

Cheong could not speak because she was choking with tears.

In the place of her silence, Sim-bongsa decided to tell her about his dream.

"In my dream last night, I saw you going somewhere in a palanquin. Since only people in high positions could ride in palanquins, the dream must be projecting that you would be a person of importance."

Breaking out in a cry, Cheong fell into her father's lap.

"Father, today I am being taken away as a sacrifice for the people of a ship. After today, I cannot see you anymore. I sent three hundred sacks of rice to Temple Mongeun-sa. Even in my absence, you should gain your sight and meet a good woman and get married and live happily."

Sim-bongsa was distraught and his face became pale.

"What in the world are you saying, Cheong? What good is it to gain sight by killing my own child? No, Cheong. You cannot go! Hey, people of the village, please stop my daughter Cheong!"

Leaving behind her crying father, Cheong followed the ship's crew aboard. After traveling for a long time, the ship began to shake greatly. Finally, they arrived at the sea of Indangsu.

Cheong prayed for a final time on the far edge of the ship where waves were breaking. "I pray and pray. I now give my life. Please be satisfied with my devotion and give sight to my father." Then, she covered her face with her white skirt and jumped into the water. Miraculously, the roaring waves came to a stop.

Once under the water, Cheong lost her consciousness and fell forever deep into the sea. When she opened her eyes, she found herself inside a majestic palace sparkling with all kinds of lights.

"Dear lady, welcome to the underwater palace."

Maids dressed in fine dresses helped her get up as if they had been waiting for her and led her into a spacious and dazzling chamber. Seated inside the chamber were the underwater king with a crown on his head and a lady beside him.

"Where, where is this place? Am I dead or alive?"

Hearing Cheong's words, the underwater king laughed out loud.

"The emperor of the kingdom of heaven was deeply moved by your filial piety and commanded that you should live."

The lady who was seated next to the underwater king ran over to where Cheong was and gazed at Cheong with her eyes filled with tears and said, "My daughter Cheong, I am your mother."

"Mother? Are you really my mother?"

Cheong and Lady Gwak embraced each other and broke out in tears.

"To be separated from you within one week of your birth, I was crushed by grief. Even in heaven, there was not a single day I spent without tears. Now, the emperor of the kingdom of heaven allowed me to meet you."

"Mother, I so desperately wanted to see you even in my dreams. But I could not picture your face in my mind! Now, I can see

44

your face."

Happily, the mother and the daughter spent several days of blissfulness together. However, she had to return to the heavenly kingdom because the time period granted to Lady Gwak had ended.

"Cheong, until we meet again in the future, you must live happily. Do you understand?"

After reluctantly parting with her mother, Cheong was able to return to land with the assistance of the underwater king.

The crew of the ship that threw Cheong into the sea as an offering was successful in their business venture and was on their way home.

As the ship was passing through the sea of Indangsu, people on board spotted a huge flower floating around in the middle of the sea.

"A flower in the middle of the sea? And the mysterious fragrance. It cannot be a common flower."

The people of the ship fetched the flower and brought it to the king.

The king was impressed by the beautiful flower that was as large as a wheel of a wagon.

"I have never seen a flower like this in my life. It is neither the flower of a Cercidiphyllum tree nor a peach flower. I am sure that it is a lotus flower that descended from heaven."

The king approached and caressed the tender petal of the flower. At once, like magic, the flower opened up widely and a virgin appeared out of it. This, of course, was Cheong.

Cheong gently got up and bowed respectfully to the king. The king's heart was beholden by Cheong's fair face and gentle demeanor. The king thought that this virgin that came out of the flower must be his companion that was sent to him by heaven.

Some time later, Cheong and the king wed and she became the queen.

As the queen, Cheong was dearly loved both by the king and the people, and she lived many blissful days. However, her thoughts always remained with her father.

The king sent his servants to the village of Dohwa to bring Sim-bongsa to him. Unfortunately, it had been a long time since Sim-bongsa left his house and there was no one who knew of his whereabouts.

Cheong was overwhelmed by sadness and worry that she could

not do anything. The king wanted so desperately to do whatever was necessary for his beloved queen. So, he commanded that all the blind men of the land should be invited to a three-day banquet at the palace.

Meanwhile, Sim-bongsa, who was grieving over the loss of his daughter, remarried a woman named Ppaengdeok Uhmum. She was greedy and spent money lavishly, and from the beginning was only interested in Sim-bongsa's money. Her money spending was so wasteful that after a while, she had spent all the money Sim-bongsa had received for Cheong's ransom.

"I've wasted all the money I'd earned by selling my daughter, and now have to make a living by begging. How am I to live with such shame?"

Sim-bongsa gathered all his remaining wealth and left the village with Ppaengdeok Uhmum.

Sim-bongsa and Paengdeok Uhmum had been moving around from this village to that, when they heard about the banquet for blind people hosted by the palace. On the way to the palace, the couple met a blind man called Hwang-bongsa. He was also on his way to the banquet. Sim-bongsa was glad that he found a friend to travel with.

As they came near the palace, Sim-bongsa looked for a stream to maybe wash himself. But when he returned after bathing, his wife had disappeared with Hwang-bongsa, taking Sim-bongsa's clothes with her. Ppaengdeok Uhmum had lured Hwang-bongsa, who was younger and had more money than Sim-bongsa, and they had run away together. Sim-bongsa, with the help of a passerby, could barely find clothes to cover himself with.

The news about the banquet spread to all the corners of the land. On the third day of the banquet for the blind, the palace yard was filled with blind men that came from all across the land. Hoping that her father was present, Cheong came to the place of banquet everyday and carefully examined the face of each blind person. However, as the end of the banquet approached, there was no sign of her father.

"Could it be that he died from the grief over my death at the sea of Indangsu? Or could it be that he finally gained his sight thanks to the offering of three hundred sacks of rice?"

"My queen, there is still some time left. Why don't we wait a little more?" The king tried to comfort Cheong.

At that moment, a blind man in the appearance of an unsightly beggar was spotted.

48

"Who are you and where do you live?"

"I am a homeless man without a name."

"Don't you have any family?"

"I lost my wife many years ago. My only child sold herself to a group of sea-faring people believing that doing so would bring sight to my eyes."

"Though I came here for the banquet for the blind, how can I, a person who became blinded by the desire to gain sight and sold his child for that purpose, be worthy to be seated at the banquet? Just let me die."

Only after she heard the words of Sim-bongsa, she was able to recognize her father.

Though she almost could not recognize him because of his ragged clothes, bone-protruding face, and completely gray hair, it was surely her father. Breaking out in tears, Cheong grabbed Sim-bongsa's hand.

"Father, it is Cheong! Your daughter that died at the sea of Indangsu came back alive!"

Sim-bongsa was stunned and asked, "What? My daughter Cheong is alive? Is that true? My dear Cheong! Let me see my daughter's face!"

As he touched Cheong's face, Sim-bongsa opened his eyes wide.

At that moment, the unthinkable happened.

Sim-bongsa's view began to lighten up and he could see the world! Hearing that Sim-bongsa gained his sight, the blind men that were sitting around in close distance began to gain sight themselves, too.

"My daughter is so beautiful. I see that my beautiful and nice daughter has become the queen!"

"Father!"

Sim-bongsa and Cheong embraced each other for a long time.

Cheong, then, brought her father to the palace and began taking care and serving him happily ever after.

Learn More......

Why did the Buddhist monks go around houses beating on the Mok-tak?

The practice of the Buddhist monks going around houses, receiving food and some money is called *tak-bal* religious begging. The monks who practiced *tak-bal* were called *tak-bal-seung* or *hwa-ju-seung*. The practice of giving charitable offerings to a *hwa-ju-seung* was called *gong-yang* offering. The monks practiced *tak-bal* as a way of disciplining themselves in humility and Buddhist believers practiced *gong-yang* to collect merit of their own.

How was a *hwa-ju-seung* dressed on his or her way to *tak-bal*? The monk wore *jang-sam*, a long gray outer robe over his or her traditional Korean undergarment. A long cloth-sack called *ba-rang* was lifted up over his or her back and shoulders. The collected offerings were placed in this sack. The monk wore straw-shoes called *jip-sin* and held *yum-ju* prayer beads and a *mok-tak* in his or her hands. *Yum-ju* and *mok-tak* are the two best-known religious items of Buddhism. *Yum-ju* were worn around the neck or wrists, or moved around the hand with fingers. The *mok-tak* is a handheld percussion instrument for chanting. The monk would beat on the *mok-tak* as he or she recited Buddhist prayers. Depending on the weather, the monk would wear a *sat-gat* an oval shaped bamboo hat.

Costume of Buddhist monks

Sat-gat

Yum-ju

Ba-rang

Mok-tak

Jang-sam

Jip-sin

Heung-Bu Jeon

The Story of Heung-Bu

The Story of Heung-Bu is a story about love between two brothers. Along with a love story, *The Story of Chun-Hyang*, and a story about devotion to one's parents, *The Story of Sim Cheong*, *The Story of Heung-Bu* completes the triology of *Pansori* stories. Every single one of these stories is not only enjoyable, but educational, making them some of the most well-known stories in Korea.

The context of *The Story of Heung-Bu* is set during the later part of the Joseon Dynasty in a village that is the meeting point of Chungcheong Province, Jeolla Province, and Gyeongsang Province. During the later part of the Joseon Dynasty, the economy was no longer solely dependent on agriculture, and commerce began to slowly expand. Because of this, people that were neither the *yangban* class nor the high class had the opportunity to make money and become rich.

It is said that if some people could become rich, other people could become very poor as well. *The Story of Heung-Bu*, though it is a story about a rich older brother and a poor younger brother, is also a story about the rich and the poor of that period. It is also a story about those who did not know how to be generous in proportion of their wealth.

The older brother, Nol-Bu, was a rich man but was unpleasant and inconsiderate to the needs of others. On the other hand, the younger brother, Heung-Bu, although he was very poor, was a good man who went out of his way to help his neighbors in need. One thing that is for sure is when one lives with a kind heart, everything will be paid back in full. At the end, Heung-Bu becomes very rich whereas Nol-Bu gets punished. Then, Nol-Bu regrets his wrongdoings and Heung-Bu supports him so that they can live well together. The themes of *The Story of Heung-Bu*, which are about brotherly love and victory over evil, were considered the greatest merits by our ancestors.

There's a saying in Korean–"There is no younger brother that is better than his older brother"–that is, no matter how well off the little sibling may be, he or she can never exceed the tolerance of the older one. But perhaps the tale of Heung-Bu and Nol-Bu will help you see that this is not always the case.

In a village where Chungcheong Province, Jeolla Province, and Gyeongsang Province meet, lived two brothers with the last name of Yeon. Older brother Nol-Bu and younger brother Heung-Bu, even though from the same mother, had very different appearances as well as personalities.

Older brother Nol-Bu was greedy and did not give an inch of sympathy for others. Every bit of what Nol-Bu did was so against common sense of morals that people whispered that Nol-Bu must have five organs and *seven* inner organs instead of the usual six, with his greed making up for the extra bit of guts.

Nol-Bu was notorious around his parts for: singing at funerals, fanning at fires, driving a stake into a growing watermelon, throwing stones at jars of soy sauce, feeding poop to a crying child, forcing a person in mid-poo to sit on his butt, slapping an innocent person's face, running away without paying for his tab, cursing, and fighting.

Heung-Bu, on the other hand, was different from his older brother. He had a kind heart and was diligent. He got along with his neighbours and volunteered for the most difficult jobs. Everyone liked him.

Nol-Bu and Heung-Bu lived together while their parents were alive, but once they passed away, Nol-Bu, as if having waited for it, called Heung-Bu and said,

"What our father has left behind to the oldest son of this household is rightfully mine. Take your family, get out, and figure out a way to live for yourselves."

With that, he took all of their father's money, land, house, and livestock, and kicked Heung-Bu out of the house. Heung-Bu, disturbed at his brother's behavior, grabbed ahold of him.

"Brother, where can I take my wife and children on such a short notice? Please, let us go after winter passes."

But Nol-Bu would not hear of it. He screamed, "That is none of my business. Get out, now!"

With no other option, good-hearted Heung-Bu took his wife and children and got out of the house empty handed. Fortunately, they were able to find an abandoned mud hut, which they were able to call home.

Having been kicked out of the house with absolutely nothing, Heung-Bu took whatever job he could get. But because he had nothing to begin with, and his family continued to grow, they could not avoid hunger for even a day. Finally, one day, it even became difficult to have a bowl of watered-down porridge.

Heung-Bu's wife, no longer able to endure the hunger, said to him, "The children are crying with hunger but we don't even have a grain of rice. Honey, please go to your brother's house and beg him for some rice."

Heung-Bu could not bear seeing his children starve, and went over to his brother's house.

When Heung-Bu walked into the house through the front door, Nol-Bu opened the door of his warm room with a pipe still in his mouth. As soon as Heung-Bu saw his brother, he got down on his knees and begged,

"Brother, I have come bearing shame because my children are about to die from starvation. Please, think of the affection you have for your brother, and please lend me a bag of rice. I will work diligently and pay it back when spring comes."

Blinking his eyes, Nol-Bu replied, "I do not know who you are."

"Brother, why are you saying such things? Do you not know your own brother Heung-Bu, the one who used to live with you just a few years ago?" Heung-Bu said, shocked.

Nol-Bu got up and yelled, "Get out of my house, wretch! How dare you enter this house again?"

"Brother, my children are dying of starvation. Please, just a *mal* Korean unit of measure which is about 18 liters of wheat..."

"I see you're not going to listen to talk. Maybe this club will change your mind!"

Nol-Bu ran out to the yard, grabbed a club that was in the corner of the house, and hit Heung-Bu with it brutally. Heung-Bu screamed in pain. At that sound, Nol-Bu's wife stopped scooping rice and came out of the kitchen. Heung-Bu, glad to see his sister-in-law, grabbed ahold of her.

"Please, sister-in-law! Please lend me a scoop of wheat!"

Startled, Nol-Bu's wife shook him away, saying, "How dare a man touch a married woman! Let this hot spoon teach you a lesson!"

With the spoon she'd used to scoop rice, Nol-Bu's wife slapped

Heung-Bu's face, hard.

Heung-Bu saw sparks fly before his eyes. But what pleased him in spite of the pain was the smell of the rice that was on the spoon. Touching his cheek, now red and swollen, he found a few rice grains stuck there. Devouring the rice stuck on his cheek, Heung-Bu said,

"Sister-in-law, let my children taste just a little bit of rice. Please slap my other cheek too."

At that plea, Nol-Bu's wife ran back into the kitchen, wiped the spoon clean of any rice, and slapped Heung-Bu's other cheek hard.

Heung-Bu returned home with not even a handful of wheat and his body black and blue with bruises. Having desperately waited for her husband to return with food, Heung-Bu's wife was shaken at Heung-Bu's state. She asked, "What is this? What happened to your face?"

"Well, it..."

"Did your brother not give you any food?"

"No, no. My brother gave me a warm bowl of rice and a drink. He gave me some food and money, but... I ran into a robber on the way home."

Heung-Bu, unable to tell his wife what happened, made up excuses.

But Heung-Bu's wife knew Nol-Bu's ill nature, and could not believe a word Heung-Bu was saying. Turning her back, she wiped tears off her face.

Heung-Bu and his family barely survived the cold and starving winter. Spring finally came.

A pair of swallows, having returned from the South, began to build a nest under the attic of Heung-Bu's house. Having made a cozy nest from soft mud and straws, the swallows laid eggs and kept them there. When the baby swallows were born, their parents began to raise them handsomely, finding food and feeding it to their children.

"There are six baby swallows in all!"

"Look, the mom is giving them bugs to eat!"

Heung Bu's children forgot all about their hunger and enjoyed watching the swallows.

One day, the swallows began to cry out loud. When Heung-Bu looked up, he saw that a huge snake was crawling up the roof to get to the nest. Among the chaos, one of the baby swallows fell from its nest.

Heung-Bu quickly grabbed a stick and chased the snake away with it. When he scooped up the baby swallow from the ground, he saw that it was alive but one of its legs had been broken.

"You poor thing! You're just a little animal. I'll take care of you."

Heung-Bu took a small piece of cloth, wrapped the swallow's leg with it, and tied it up with a fine thread. For a few days, Heung-Bu took very good care of it.

In about ten days, the baby swallow's leg was healed. Heung-Bu's family protected the swallows' nest so that they could live at ease. When fall came and the baby swallows had grown, they flew down to the South.

The next spring, when swallows began to return from the South one by one, Heung-Bu's children, looking at the empty nest, wondered, "Will the swallows that had nested above our house return?"

"What do you think happened to the swallow that broke its leg last spring?"

At that moment, a swallow began to circle above the front yard.

"Look at its leg! That's the swallow I took care of last spring! I'm sure of it!" said Heung-Bu joyfully.

After circling the yard a few times, the swallow dropped what it was holding in its mouth. It was a calabash seed.

Heung-Bu grabbed the seed the swallow had given him and planted it under the fence. It began to sprout in just a few days, and its branches grew. It absorbed the sweet rain and the cool breeze of the summer, and finally, produced three ripe calabashes. Heung-Bu and his wife were greatly pleased at the size of the calabashes.

"I have never seen calabashes that big! They must be full and ripe inside too, right?"

"Let's boil them up and eat what's inside. We can dry the skin and sell it. It looks like these calabashes will help us get by this *Chuseok* Korean Thanksgiving Day after all!" said Heung-Bu, as he climbed up to the roof and brought the calabashes down.

64

With the ripe and yellow calabash in the middle, Heung-Bu and his wife began to cut it up.

Slowly, carefully, let us saw
Hey, ho, let us saw
Let's open this calabash
Boil up and eat the inside
As for the skin,
We can dry it,
And carry rice and water with it

When the children saw Heung-Bu sing excitedly, they also sang along,

"Hey, ho, let us saw."

All of a sudden, the calabash split open in half with a loud bang. And from the inside, a little boy walked out slowly. He was wearing bright blue clothes.

The little boy handed a small plate with mysterious medicines to the dumbfounded Heung-Bu.

"Inside this bottle of white gem is a drink that will bring a dead person back to life; the medicine that's on this plate will let the blind see, the deaf hear, and the mute speak. The medicine

that's wrapped in this paper will let one live forever in youth. These medicines cannot be found anywhere on earth. Their value is absolutely priceless. Use them wisely."

With that, the boy disappeared into thin air.

Inside the calabash from which the boy emerged were two boxes made of wood. When they opened it, they found that one box was full of rice, and the other, money.

How long has it been since they saw rice! Heung-Bu's wife poured the rice out of the box and cooked it. With the money, she bought ingredients and made side dishes. With that, the family ate plentifully, something they had not been able to do in a long time.

What's even more amazing was that the boxes never ran out of rice and money, no matter how much they took from them!

Elated, Heung-Bu and his wife opened the second calabash.

With a bang, the calabash this time showered all kinds of gold, silver, and other precious jewels down on the family like rain. Not only that, the calabash kept producing silks with beautiful colors, sleek furniture, books, and kitchen appliances. Heung-Bu and his family danced with joy. Everyone in the family, excited, touched the jewels of different colors and shapes, and wrapped the soft silk around their body.

When they opened the third calabash, carpenters and sculptors, and male and female servants made their way out. They soon began to carry in wood and stones on wagons, and built a house.

In a matter of seconds, Heung-Bu's house of mud disappeared. Before them now was a house of ninety-nine rooms. In their new house, they brought in their new furniture, rice, money, and gold and silver. Heung-Bu could not believe his eyes, and wondered if this were all a dream.

The news that Heung-Bu's family, who had been starving right until yesterday, had now become a millionaire overnight, reached the village very quickly. The news finally reached the ears of Nol-Bu. Nol-Bu was very curious as to how his poor brother could have become so rich so quickly. Wanting to rid Heung-Bu of his newfound wealth, Nol-Bu immediately went to him.

"Heung-Bu, you wretch, how did you accumulate so much wealth? Who did you steal from? Tell me the truth, now!"

"Brother, what do you mean, steal? That's not how it happened."

Heung-Bu went on to tell Nol-Bu of the things that had happened to him.

Hearing that Heung-Bu had become rich by taking care of a swallow with a broken leg, Nol-Bu rejoiced to himself that he could also become wealthy by doing the same.

Nol-Bu hurried home, and mashing some mud and a lot of straw, Nol-Bu built a nest on his roof. He then ran this way and that, trying to catch swallows. Finally, a pair of swallows went into the nest Nol-Bu had built and laid eggs.

After the baby swallows were born and had grown a little, Nol-Bu took one of them out from the nest and snapped one of its fragile legs, breaking it. Then Nol-Bu wrapped the leg with a cloth and a thread.

The next spring, a swallow also brought Nol-Bu a calabash seed.

When Nol-Bu planted the seed under the fence, the plant grew all summer long, and finally bore ten calabashes that were as big and ripe as the full moon. Nol-Bu greatly rejoiced, dancing with excitement.

"Yes! Heung-Bu only had three calabashes, but I'm getting ten!"

With the ripe and yellow calabash in the middle, Nol-Bu and his wife began to cut it open.

Slowly, carefully, let us saw
Hey, ho, let us saw
When this calabash bears
Money, gold, silver and jewels,
Shall we build a house of gold
Even the millionaire of China would be envious of?

Finally, the calabash split open in half. From its inside, an old man walked out. When he saw Nol-Bu, he suddenly yelled at him.

"Nol-Bu, you wretch, your father and mother were once servants of my house, who ran away later. I ran here because I heard that you were a rich man. Here is a sack; give me the money for your parents!"

Then, from the calabash, strong men came out with sticks and ropes, and surrounded Nol-Bu. Nol-Bu, greatly abashed, began to put money in the sack.

But no matter how much money Nol-Bu put in the sack, it would not be filled. Nol-Bu put in the entire money chest; it swallowed it whole. He put in hundreds of bags of rice. Again, it swallowed them.

Running out of patience, Nol-Bu began to beg the old man.

"Old man, I have put in everything I own. But the sack will not fill up. What more do you expect me to do?"

"Your sincerity is lacking a great deal, but I shall retire for today. When I decide that you have not given me enough, I shall return."

With that, the old man and the men disappeared into thin air, like smoke.

Nol-Bu, having lost his money, opened the second calabash to regain some of his possessions.

But from the second calabash came out hundreds of beggars, who took over his house. Lying around his bedroom, the front yard, and everywhere else, they began to demand rice and drinks. They then proceeded to turn the house upside down. When Nol-Bu gave the beggars every last one of his possessions, they disappeared into the calabash.

Nol-Bu's wife, upset and worried, tried to stop her husband.

"Honey, I do not think these calabashes have anything good for us. Let us not open any more. Let's just throw them out."

"What are you talking about? We overcame small obstacles with the first two, so now we shall be rewarded with great things with the other calabashes. *Now*, we'll get sacks upon sacks of blessings and gold."

But such luck did not find its way to Nol-Bu.

Mourners came out from the third calabash, who tried to bury Nol-Bu alive by putting him into a coffin. From the fourth, poisonous snakes and serpents jumped out and nearly traumatized the souls out of Nol-Bu and his wife. Barely getting rid of the snakes, Nol-Bu opened yet another calabash, which revealed a golden light from within.

"Honey, that golden light must be from the gold!"

The two were looking intently at the calabash, when all of a sudden the golden water of urine and feces flowed out like a fountain and soaked their bodies through and through. In a matter of seconds, the house began to smell of something awful.

Every time they opened a calabash, they were robbed of their possessions. The original state of their house could no longer be found.

With every single one of their servants having run away, Nol-Bu and his wife were completely exhausted. But Nol-Bu could not resist opening up the last calabash.

"Honey, please do not open the last calabash. What will you do if something even worse happened?"

Nol-Bu could not be persuaded even by his wife's words. He opened the last calabash.

When the calabash opened, hundreds of soldiers came out and surrounded them. The leader of the soldiers, gigantic in size, put a sword to Nol-Bu's neck and declared,

"Listen, greedy Nol-Bu. It was not enough for you to treat your innocent brother badly and kick him out of your house. You also had to break the leg of an innocent animal. Even after that, do you wish to live? Considering all your sins, you should be killed on the spot. But I will let you live, provided you repent of your old ways and live in harmony with your brother. Will you do that?"

The general's thunderous voice echoed throughout the place and Nol-Bu could no longer hold his own. He bowed down, with his body completely on the floor. With big tears flowing down his face, he asked for forgiveness.

"I finally see all the wrongs I have done. I have sinned greatly, but please, forgive me just this once. From now on, I will live in harmony with my brother and do good deeds for my neighbours. I will live like a decent human being."

"I will go, trusting that you will act upon your word. Keep your promise!" With this, the general and the soldiers disappeared like a wind.

Heung-Bu, having heard that Nol-Bu had experienced a great

disaster by opening up his calabashes, came to him. Nol-Bu knelt before Heung-Bu and sincerely asked for his forgiveness for the wrongs he had done to him.

Heung-Bu took his brother and sister-in-law into his home, washing them and giving them good clothes to wear. For his brother, now nothing but a beggar, Heung-Bu gave half of his possessions. There was no one who was not inspired by Heung-Bu's kind heart.

What is *Pansori*?

The Story of Chun-Hyang, *The Story of Sim Cheong*, and *The Story of Heung-Bu* are the stories that belong to the types of *Pansori*. Originally passed on orally from generation to generation, these stories were accepted into *Pansori* during the late Joseon Dynasty and reorganized as written novels later on.

Pansori is a type of folk music native to Korea. *Pansori* consists primarily of a single narrator who combines storytelling and singing in the same beat to the rhythms of a drum and uses this environment to communicate the story to the audience. Because emotions and dramatic circumstances were expressed through songs in the plot stage, it aided the listeners to experience the drama realistically.

These stories did maintain the rhythmic nature because they were once songs and then later were ultimately written down. The reason that they are classified as 'novels in the *Pansori*' and different from traditional novels is due to the presence of this rhythmic nature. Particularly, *The*

Story of Heung-Bu is loved by many because it contains many fun and interesting scenes such as that of Heung-Bu slicing the giant fruit shells to the rhythms of the song he was singing, the scene of all kinds of jewels and treasures falling out of these shells, and the scene of body wastes slowly flowing out of Nol-Bu's fruit shells.

Pansori

Ong Go-Jib Jeon

The Story of Ong Go-Jib

The Story of Ong Go-Jib is the last novel in the *Pansori* tradition that we will read. Unlike the previous three novels in the *Pansori* tradition, *Pansori* for Ong Go-Jib was not passed down. It is the story about a rich man named Ong Go-Jib belonging to the *yangban* class. Ong Go-Jib pays dearly for the trouble when he meets someone who pretends to be him and later becomes a different person as a result. The wicked character of Ong Go-Jib is very similar to that of Nol-Bu in *The Story of Heung-Bu.*

The historical setting is during the later part of Joseon Dynasty. The main character, Ong Go-Jib, was not of the highest class, but he was a man of great influence in the region because he had great wealth. In the later part of the Joseon Dynasty, we see many people like him who became rich through other means than power. Although these people had great wealth and positions of power, they did not show personal character that matched their reputation. *The Story of Ong Go-Jib* shows the irony about such people.

Spatial context is set in Ongjin Valley of Ongdang Village. It seems these are not real places but imaginary places within the story. Don't you feel that there is kind of a rhyming pattern in 'Ong Go-Jib who lived in Ongjin Valley of Ongdang Village'? Does it not seem like these places were made intentionally to fit the name of the main character?

We describe a person who does not change his or her opinions but remains stubborn as having 'really strong *go-jib*'. Likewise, to put the negative light on someone who is stubborn, we say he or she is '*Ong Go-Jib*'. Precisely, the terminology was borrowed from this novel.

Do you remember that the central theme of *The Story of Heung-Bu* was the idea that good people end up blessed and bad people are punished at the end of the day? Ong Go-Jib carries a similar theme. However, we see that even Nol-Bu and Ong Go-Jib were forgiven and comforted when they repented of their past wrongdoings. I believe it was the belief of our ancestors that there is no one who does not change, or remains bad until the end. Anyone who repents of his or her actions can always be forgiven.

Now, we shall examine how Ong Go-Jib's wicked character changes before him.

Once upon a time, a person with the last name Ong lived in Ongjin Valley of Ongdang Village. He was known for being very stubborn ^{having a strong *go-jib*} and his tendency was to do whatever he wished. Koreans often say a stubborn person has strong "*go-jib*." People called him, "Ong Go-Jib." In addition, his personality was so terrible that there was no one who liked him. At the sight of Ong Go-Jib approaching from afar, people would quietly avoid him by taking a path away from him.

Despite this, no one knows how, but he was the richest man in the village. All kinds of treasure were piled up in every room of his palace-like mansion and his storage was filled with all kinds of grains.

Though he was so rich that he lacked nothing, he was very stingy, even to his parents. When his mother, in her eighties, became bedridden because of an illness, he did not even make chicken soup with chicken meat or bring her one bag of medicine. More disgracefully, because of the cost of heating the room, he made her stay in a freezing cold room even in winter time.

One day, his mother cried bitterly,

"My son, Ong Go-Jib, don't you know how I cherished you like a treasure when raising you? How come you do not understand that grace? In the old times, I heard that a certain son served his parents by catching a carp fish out of icy water. Forget about carp fish. Instead, you mistreat me like this!"

But Ong Go-Jib was not about to be moved by these words.

"Even Emperor Qin Shi Huangdi of Ancient China who ruled over the world wished to live a thousand years, but he died not even living one hundred years. Even Hegemon-King of Western Chu, Xiang Yu, who won every time he went to war, killed himself upon losing a battle. Then, how come you fear death after having lived your life in its whole? Isn't there an ancient saying that it is a rarity to live up to seventy years of age? Since you, my mother, have already reached the age of eighty, you should not think it is unfair even if you die immediately."

If this is how he treated his mother, then it should be clear to anyone how he dealt with other people. He would yell at children playing outside his house to quiet down. He would tie a lazy servant around a tree. When a beggar came to his house, he would keep the beggar hanging in front of his house for a long time by pretending as if he would really offer the beggar something. It was frequent that Ong Go-Jib would keep a guest in the guest house guessing about whether he could spend the night there or not, only to be sent away at sunset.

Of all the people, Ong Go-Jib mistreated Buddhist monks the most. Whenever the sound of *mok-tak* was heard or even the shadow of monk's robe was seen, Ong Go-Jib yelled and cursed freely at them. If that did not satisfy him, he would beat them up and kick them out. As the news of such abuse spread, no monk would even think about going near the house of Ong Go-Jib.

Around this time, there was a famous guru living at a Buddhist temple called Chwiahm-sa. He was called 'Master Hak' and possessed an admirable character as well as the ability to perform magic. One day, suddenly stopping in the middle of his meditation, he said,

"There is a man named Ong Go-Jib in Ongdang Village who is not afraid to curse Buddha and treat monks like his enemies. The cries of those monks that were mistreated even reach me here that I cannot remain still and focus on my meditation. I shall return after having punished him severely."

Master Hak put on a ragged robe that had been stitched up here and there, wore a shabby pointed straw hat, put a stained Buddhist rosary around his neck, and left on his way.

Immediately after arriving in Ongdang Village, Master Hak went straight to the house of Ong Go-Jib and began hitting his *mok-tak* and asked for alms. Alms-giving as in offering money or food to a Buddhist temple or a monk without conditions was common.

"*Na-mo-a-mi-ta-bul Gwanseeum Bosal.* Give alms to Buddha and be blessed."

A servant came running out of the house and said,

"Hey, Mister! Don't you know that my master's known for his temper and refusal to give alms? He is taking a nap right now. When he wakes up, you will surely be treated rudely let alone given alms. So, just go away right now."

However, Master Hak answered as if he was clueless,

"I don't believe that a rich household like this would treat a monk like that. There is an old saying, 'If you pile up evil deeds, certainly misfortune will follow. If you pile up good deeds, you will certainly be blessed.' I am a monk belonging to Chwiahm-sa, the temple in Wolchulbong of Mount Geumgang "The Diamond Mountains". I came out to raise funds for the temple building which is too old and worn out. Go now and tell your master to donate one thousand gold coins."

Ong Go-Jib, who was listening quietly to the conversation, ran towards the monk on barefoot and pointed his finger at him saying,

"What? One thousand gold coins? You are trying to rob me in my own house, aren't you? If people receive blessings because they give alms like you say, then who would be poor and miserable in this world? Stop selling the name of Buddha and trying to steal my wealth!"

Master Hak did not back down at all but said boldly.

"How dare you say such a thing to me! Until now, I kept my body and mind clean. I also studied the holy words day and night as well as prayed for this country and its people. What do you mean by stealing?"

The words of Master Hak had an impact of pushing Ong Go-Jib back a little bit. Ong Go-Jib said,

"It seems like you learned a thing or two from somewhere. Try then reading my face and telling me about my fortune."

People of the old used to read the contours of a person's face and assessed things such as a person's personality, fate, and length of life.

Master Hak carefully read Ong Go-Jib's face and said,

"Since your face has thin eyelashes and a broad forehead, you should have sufficient wealth but not many children. Also, your narrow face tells me that you don't listen to other people well. Since your hands and feet are small, you will die prematurely."

Ong Go-Jib became furious by these words.

"You insolent monk! How can you speak such spiteful words? Hey, Dolsae, Mongchi! Arrest that monk at once and give him hell."

The servants rushed to him and beat him senselessly and threw him out the house.

Master Hak, who was lying on the ground as if he was dead, got up after a while and shook the dirt off his clothes as if nothing had happened. All the bruises over his body disappeared completely as well.

Master Hak returned to Chwiahm-sa
and told other monks,
"I have never seen a person that
rude and ruthless.
I think I will fix him up
real good this time."
Master Hak made a scarecrow
out of a haystack. Then, he placed a
talisman on its face and began reciting a spell.
Immediately, the scarecrow turned into the exact
same appearance of Ong Go-Jib.
At once, the fake Ong Go-Jib went to Onggin Valley
in Ongdang Village and entered the house of
the real Ong Go-Jib.
"Hey! What are you doing?
Did you all sweep the yard and clean
the rooms? Did you feed the animals

in the barn? Are you being lazy because I was out of the house for a while?"

As the imposter was pushing the servants hard to do work, the real Ong Go-Jib entered the house and said, "Well, who is making a commotion in someone else's house?" The imposter replied, "Who are you to enter someone else's house and act like the owner?"

"Who are you? How come you are in someone else's house and act like the owner?" As soon as the real Ong Go-Jib saw the face of the imposter, he was shocked. Here was someone who looked, talked, and dressed like himself. The real Ong Go-Jib yelled at his servants, "Hey, you guys, what are you doing not dragging him out of the house right now? That thief is pretending to be me because he desires my wealth."

The imposter did not back down but yelled, "What? That's exactly what I am trying to say. Where did you come from, you thief? Why don't you get out of my house right now?"

The two began to argue with each other, both claiming that they were the real owner of the house. The servants did not know which side to take but remained standing with a baffled look on their faces.

The wife of Ong Go-Jib who was inside in the inner room of the house heard about the commotion outside and sent out her maid to inquire, saying,

"Not long ago, when my husband went out, he sustained a small hole on the inner garment of his robe. Only my husband and I know about this. Why don't you go and check it out and come back?"

At once, the maid ran out to where the two were and asked each to show her the inner garment of the robe. This strategy did not work because surprisingly, there was a hole on each Ong Go-Jib's robe.

Then, the daughter-in-law volunteered and went over to the

reception room.

"My father-in-law has a scar on his head and there are white strains of hair on top of it. By checking this, I would know who the real one is. So, show me your head."

The real Ong Go-Jib was happy to hear this and untied the knot on his head to show her the scar. Instantly, using magic, the imposter pulled out the white strains of hair from the real Ong Go-Jib and planted them on his head instead.

"Well, now you can see that I am your father-in-law, can't you?"

"I don't know. There is a scar but no white hair."

This time, the imposter nudged his head out. When the daughter-in-law attentively checked it, she saw white hair.

"Right, here are white strains of hair. He surely is the real father-in-law."

The real Ong Go-Jib felt so upset he felt like his insides would explode.

"No, she calls the imposter her father-in-law but does not recognize the real one! Oh my, this is so upsetting. What am I to do?"

Though Ong Go-Jib's wife joined the fray by running out from the inner room, there was no way to decide who the real one was.

The two Ong Go-Jibs agreed to go before the town magistrate to have him distinguish the real from the imposter.

Standing before the town magistrate, it was the imposter who spoke first.

"My name is Ong Go-Jib and my family has been living in Ongjin Valley of Ongdang Village for many generations. Then, that man appeared dressed like me and is trying to steal my wealth. Sir, I demand you to punish him."

Then, the real Ong Go-Jib was flabbergasted and said, "That is not correct, my lord. He is saying what I have to say. Please submit your wise verdict."

The magistrate studied them for a while but could not find any way to tell them apart. He went as far as stripping them naked and comparing them. They looked exactly the same. After deeply considering, the magistrate spoke, "Though you look alike, you must have different ancestors. Now, tell me about your ancestors."

The real Ong Go-Jib opened his mouth confidently,

"Yes, my father's name is Ong-Song and my grandfather is Man-Song. My great-grandfather..."

At this point, Ong Go-Jib found himself at a loss for words.

He did not know anymore. It was doubtful that Ong Go-Jib who had been disrespectful of his elders knew much about his family history.

Now, the imposter began to speak,

"My father is Ong-Song and he served as a general in military and my grandfather, Man-Song, served as the joint chief of staff. Speaking of my family's wealth, we harvest two thousand sacks of grains from the fields, there are six horses, twenty-two pigs, and sixty chickens. For household items, we have closets, chests, and folding screens. I keep the folding screen with the painting of a peony in the attic because I want to give it to my son. In addition, I have ten gold rings, twenty silver rings, thirty rolls of ramie fabric, and thirteen rolls of silk."

Nodding in agreement, the magistrate now asked the real Ong Go-Jib.

"You have all the good things in the world. Now, you speak. What else do you have in your house?"

The real Ong Go-Jib hesitated a little bit as he tried to think. Taking advantage of this, the imposter continued to speak,

"Besides these things, I have six pairs of leather shoes. Of them, one pair was ruined when a mouse ate into the nose of the shoe. So I placed it inside a closet. Everything I said is true and you can confirm it. If anything I said is proved to be wrong, you can beat me with a paddle to death."

In response, the magistrate invited the imposter up to the wooden floor where he was seated and said, "You are the real one! Here, take my cup and drink it."

The imposter bowed to the magistrate by lowering his forehead all the way to the floor and said, "Thank you, magistrate. If it weren't for you, I might have lost all of my wealth to that fraud. I will never forget this grace of yours even if I die."

Happy to hear these words, the magistrate laughed contently and commanded his soldiers,

"That imposter took over the possessions of another person out of greed. Immediately, give him a beating of thirty lashes and kick him out! If he still claims to be the real one, then give him additional one hundred lashes."

When he received thirty lashes, the real Ong Go-Jib was almost dead.

"You insolent, would you still claim that you are the real Ong Go-Jib?"

Fearing that he would die while receiving one hundred lashes, Ong Go-Jib begged and shook his head. "No, sir, I am so sorry. I was blind by my greed and lied. Please forgive me."

"From now on, do not even come near this village. If I see you again, then surely you will not avoid death."

In the matter of one day, he lost his wealth and family. He became dirt poor and an outlaw.

"This is because of all the sins I committed. I want to see my elderly mother and beautiful wife. If I were given a chance to go back, I would serve my mother with devotion and be good to my wife and family."

On the other hand, the fake Ong Go-Jib returned home successfully. His wife, son, and daughter-in-law all came out to greet him. Ong Go-Jib said to them,

"I almost lost all of my wealth and family. In the past, I knew how to hang onto my wealth but did not know how to share it with others. From now on, I am going to distribute my wealth and grains to help those in need and look after the sick."

His family and servants rejoiced over the transformed Ong Go-Jib.

A long time had passed, while the imposter lived in luxury at home, the real Ong Go-Jib suffered so much as he lived as a beggar begging for food from others.

"Oh my, miserable me. Having lost all my wealth, my family,

I have to live like this... for why should I go on living? I wish I were dead..."

Ong Go-Jib walked for a long time lamenting about his place in life. Before he knew it, he entered a valley in Mount Geumgang. As he moved deeper into the woods, he found clear water flowing in a stream in the deep valley which was situated between the high mountain peaks. Ong Go-Jib was fascinated by the beautiful scenery and kept going deeper until he came to rest and cooled down a little on a rock.

The woods were packed with trees and many pairs of mountain birds were flying around. Beautiful flowers with unknowable names were in bloom all over the place. Ong Go-Jib thought about his home and became tearful.

"How great would it be only if I could turn back time! I would be a new person and live as a decent human being..."

At that moment, Ong Go-Jib felt someone was around and saw an old man with all white hair seated on a rock. He immediately perceived that the old man was not an ordinary person. The old man said,

"It does not matter for you to regret now. Who can you blame since you are being punished for your own wrongdoings?"

Realizing that the old man was talking about him, Ong Go-Jib ran to him at once and knelt before him.

"I know I deserve to die ten thousand times when I think about all the wrongs that I did. But please give me one more chance. Please let me die after seeing my sick mother and wife and children one more time. This is my last wish." Ong Go-Jib pled with the old man tearfully.

"You, no good human! Will you still make your elderly mother in her eighties sleep in a cold room and mistreat her? Will you again harass those monks who serve Buddha? I could care less to have you put to death. But since you are deeply regretful of how you lived in the past, I will make an exception and forgive you. When you return home, be a new person and live nobly."

After saying these things, the old man wrote him a talisman and handed it to him. "Put this on your body and return home. Then everything will turn back the way it was." As soon as he finished speaking, the old man disappeared into thin air.

At once, Ong Go-Jib returned to his house with the talisman. When he opened the gate and entered, his wife who was sitting on the wooden floor appalled and yelled out. "Dear! Come out here and see. That con man is here again."

Ong Go-Jib's wife ran to the reception room where the fake Ong Go-Jib had been staying and jerked the door open.

However, Ong Go-Jib was nowhere to be found but in his place a doll that was made out of hay was lying around. The servants, the son, and the daughter-in-law also came out.

"Dear, I am back. I am the real Ong Go-Jib, your husband."

Ong Go-Jib explained to them everything that he went through. Then, he promised to change his heart and become a new person. All the family members were so astonished that they could not keep their mouths closed.

"In the past, I was Ong Go-Jib who spent time doing bad deeds and being nasty. But from now on, I will live virtuously and be stubborn in doing good deeds.

Only then, the wife smiled and welcomed Ong Go-Jib warmly. From then on, Ong Go-Jib became a good person and served his mother in devotion and lived happily ever after.

What did a *yangban*'s residence during the Joseon Dynasty look like?

Han-ok is a term that describes Korean traditional houses. From the layout of a *han-ok*, one can gather the thoughts of an old Korean who values ancestor worship and the separation of men and women.

The most important part of a *han-ok* was the shrine. *Yangbans* took much care to build shrines inside their residences in order to be able to worship their ancestors. Today, it is normal to pay tribute to one's ancestors only on certain days. But back then, it was normal to build a shrine in the courtyard of the house and pay tribute to ancestors every morning. Also, within the residence, there was a guest house which was the proper territory of men and the inner chamber was the proper territory of women.

At the entrance of a *yangban's* residence stood the tall main gate displaying the respected status of that *yangban* household. Past the gate stood the servants' quarters and the guest house. One had to pass a door or two to get to the women's quarters located in the inner chamber.

Surrounded by other buildings and walls, it was impossible to see the inner chamber from the outside. The servants' quarters were strategically placed between the guest house and the inner chamber so that it would be convenient for servants to serve the master and his wife.

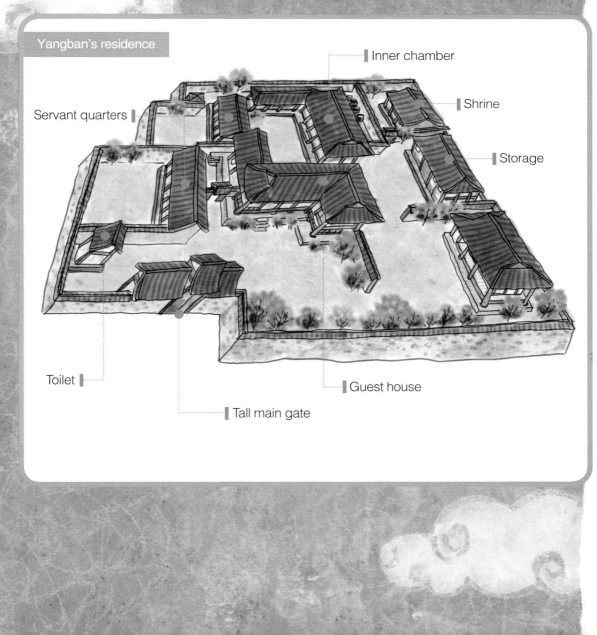

Yangban's residence

Inner chamber

Shrine

Servant quarters

Storage

Toilet

Guest house

Tall main gate

Yangban Jeon

The Story of Yangban

The stories that were introduced so far are the ones that were popular among people of the common class. This time, we shall examine a story of the *yangbans* ^{upper class} who lived during the same time period.

The Story of Yangban along with *The Story of Heo-Saeng* is a representative novel of the type that ridicules *yangbans* written in Chinese characters. Though the author of the novel, Park Ji-Won (1737–1805), was of the *yangban* class, it contains criticism of how *yangbans* were in his time.

The description of the *yangban* in *The Story of Yangban* is someone who is incapable of adapting to the changes around him. To him, saving face was more important than anything he could imagine, doing neither business nor farm work with his own hands. Without the ability to pay, he kept on borrowing grain from the government. When his debt became uncontrollable, he just looked to heaven for help. This part exposes the reality of incapable and irresponsible *yangbans* very well.

In this way, some *yangbans* became poor. On the other hand, as agricultural techniques improved and commerce developed, a new class of rich individuals began to emerge from middle class and commoners. Often, these people had the desire even to pay for high status.

Economically suffering *yangbans* needed money and people with significant wealth needed status. This union of needs led to buying and selling of status as well as family registry, which was the basis for claiming socio-cultural class.

The *yangban* character in this story also wanted to sell his status because of his poverty. The author criticizes the people of the *yangban* class for hopelessly clinging onto status and outward appearance, and not working hard to support themselves.

.

Once, there lived a '*yangban*' in the Jeongseon County of Gangwon Province. He was wise in character and enjoyed reading. The people in the district respected him as a *seonbi*–scholar–for his deep knowledge and high morals. If a new government official came into office in the district, they were willing to go find this *yangban* to greet him and receive his welcome. But what use was it to have much knowledge if he struggled to gain a meal each day, for his family was extremely poor?

At that time, there was a *hwangok* system in Joseon. Portions of grain would be given in the spring, when there was no harvest, from the government storage. In return, the people would have to give back the portion with added interest after the harvest in the fall.

This '*yangban*' was kept alive by borrowing grain, for he had no other means of earning a living. His debt grew larger as seasons passed, as snow gathered into a snowball, until he owed a thousand *seoks* an old traditional measuring unit used in Korea. His debt was huge.

One day, the governor of Gangwon Province was making his rounds in the district, and arrived near Jeongseon. He was enraged when he looked over the grain distribution records.

"Who is this man who has borrowed all this grain, and still has no thought of paying it back? Who does he think he is? Go and bring him here!"

The officer who had been sent knew the *yangban*'s situation too well to arrest him. But he was between a rock and a hard place, since it was his superior who had given him the orders. He couldn't decide on whether to arrest the nobleman or not.

While the officer worried over his dilemma, what do you think the nobleman was doing? He couldn't come up with any means of paying such a large sum. All he could do was look up to heaven and cry bitterly. As his wife looked over this scene, she said,

"All your life you loved to sit and read, but did it ever bring you food or rice? Every day you called yourself a *yangban*, but nobility has no monetary value at all."

Fortunately, at the same time, there lived a wealthy lower class man in that area. He had lots of land and enough livestock to take care of and live in a great mansion. He possessed all that he desired except for one thing, which bothered him all the time; his low status. As a person belonging to the lower class, he had no power to change it or to buy his way to the *yangban* status.

This man heard of the *yangban* who was on the verge of being imprisoned since he had no means of paying off his debt. He thought this was his great opportunity. So he gathered his family and discussed how the *yangban* deserved what was to come.

"*Yangban*s are always respected, even if they are poor to the bone, and yet, I am always mistreated even with all my fortune because of my status as a peasant. It's ridiculous that I cannot speak up freely before a nobleman, and instead I have to move around them unnoticed. How demeaning it is that I have to bow my head so low that my nose touches the dirt of the ground, when I see a *yangban* in the distance headed in my direction."

The rich man spoke with such anguish that he squirted spit out of his mouth.

"All my life I have lived in this pathetic way, and my son and grandson must not endure the same in the future. Across the stream, on the other side of town, there is a *yangban* who might be inprisoned because he is unable to repay his debts. What if we paid off his debts instead and bought the birthrights of the *yangban*?"

"Father, this is definitely a chance that heaven has given us. Let's buy it with this opportunity and live loudly, free of misery."

The rich man's whole family was so excited that they almost got up and danced.

The rich man instantly went and found the nobleman. He proposed his trade of paying the debt and instead receiving the birthrights of a *yangban*. With the payment date approaching fast, the *yangban*, who had come up with no other plan, was greatly relieved to hear this. He assumed that it was mercy shown from heaven, and agreed to the proposition on the spot. Immediately, his bait was taken and the rich man went to the distribution office and paid off all the debts.

The next day, the governor heard that the *yangban* had paid off his debt in full. He questioned how it was possible.

"It's strange. Where did the *yangban* find funds to pay off his debts all at once when he can't even afford a meal?"

The governor was so anxious that he personally went to meet the *yangban*.

When the governor arrived at the house, it was to his surprise that the *yangban* was lying with his face down on the floor, wearing the hat and ragged clothing of a servant. He was unable to even lift his head up to the governor. It was the habit of servants to recognize their insignificance in the presence of *yangbans*.

"With what reason does the governor come to meet such an insignificant person as myself in such a filthy place?"

As the *yangban* said this with his head bowed, the governor was staggered and urged him to stand.

"Dear sir, what has made you wear such ragged clothes and say such things, as if you were a servant?"

At this, the *yangban* lowered his frame even lower to the ground and said,

"Oh, you are too generous, dear sir, that I am utterly ashamed before you. I have not lowered myself without any reason. I am merely adjusting to my servant position. By selling my *yangban* birthrights, I was able to pay off my debt at the grain storage. From now on, the rich man who paid off the debt has gained the status of a *yangban*, so how could I continue living as a nobleman?"

At that, the governor understood the whole situation. After a moment's thought, the governor came to his wits and said,

"That rich man is a smart gentleman, incomparable to any other gentlemen, a true nobleman out of all the *yangbans*. He was humble and didn't brag about his wealth, and wise in helping another man out of his struggles! And that wasn't all, he was smart enough to trade his lowly status to that of a better one. Hence, he is well deserving of his newly acquired *yangban* status!"

After the governor gave a great deal of praise to the rich man in this way, he continued his thought.

"In the midst of buying and selling your *yangban* status, you didn't make any written record of the life changing transaction, which could lead to further problems in the future. I will gather some witnesses from the village and make you a document so that there will be no trouble later on."

After returning to his office, the governor gathered some people. Hearing rumors of a new *yangban* document to be made, many townspeople gathered in packs with great curiosity. When all had gathered on the field in front of the office, the governor placed the rich man at the highest seat and the *yangban* at the lowest. Then, he began to write the document.

We make this document, in XX-day, on September, 1745:

The document below is evidence of the fact that this man has paid off the debt of a thousand sacks of grain, in trade of the birthrights of the yangban status. The newly introduced yangban needs to understand the conditions of the yangban. In general, there are many levels of the yangban status.

Those who are accustomed to reading are called seonbi the scholars; those who take positions in office are called sa-dae-bu the gentry; and those with high morals are gun-ja the gentlemen.

When greeting the king, the military nobility should stand on the west, while the noblemen with civil duties should stand on the east.

Hence, both military and civil nobilities compose the yangban class.

손으로 돈 안만지기

No touching money with hands

새벽에 책 읽기

Reading books at dawn

이웃 소 몰아다 자기 밭갈기

Driving neighbor's cow to plow your own field

화로에 손 쬐지 말기

No warming hands at fireside

안 듣는 백성 코에 물 붓기

ring water into the noses of disobedient people

Therefore, you are free to choose your certain position between the two.

The governor continued with the specific attitudes a *yangban* should possess in daily life.

A yangban should never act in a low fashion, but rather distinguish himself from the rest, learning from the ancestors. A yangban should wake up between 3 and 4 a.m. and turn on his lantern to read and educate himself. He should look beyond his nose. His ankle should be gathered under his seat when reading, and he should be able to memorize the Dongrae Bakeui a book written in 1168 in China. Everyone had to read this book to take the 'gwageo' test, the highest-level government entrance exam *with such ease that it is like a ball rolling on ice.*
He should endure hunger, endure the cold, and never speak of his own poverty.
He should make any sound with his teeth, tap the back of his head lightly to keep himself awake, always cough low, and always swallow his spit.
When putting on the skullcap or the hat of a yangban,

he must dust it off with the sleeve of his shirt, so that the watermark texture is clearly visible. When washing, he shouldn't rub the dirt off his skin too hard, and when brushing his teeth he should make no sound. When he calls on his servants, he should call them with a lull. He should walk in a slow pace, with the heel of his shoes dragging.

He should be able to recite and copy hard poetry texts, as the Dangshi Pumhwi ^{Compilation of Dang Poetry}*, writing a hundred words on each page in fine handwriting. He shouldn't touch money with his hand, and shouldn't repay the price of rice. However hot it gets, he shouldn't take his socks off. Even when eating, he should be in full attire—not forgetting his skullcap and hat.*

When eating, he should not finish the soup prior to his rice, and he shouldn't make any chewing or slurping sounds. He shouldn't press the food too hard with the ends of his chopsticks nor eat raw green onions. When drinking alcohol, he shouldn't lick his mustache, and when smoking, he shouldn't drag in a breath too large that his cheeks cave in.

He shouldn't physically hit anyone, even in high temper,

and he should not throw any breakable objects, like that of a dish. Anger should be controlled, so that he doesn't swear or beat any servants without good reason.

Even when disciplining a cow or horse, he shouldn't talk badly about the owners who trained the animal. He shouldn't call upon a shaman when ill, nor call upon a Buddhist monk when making sacrifices to the ancestors.

In the cold, he shouldn't put his hands before a furnace, and when he speaks he shouldn't spit. He shouldn't steal any cows or gamble.

If any of the stated actions is not kept precisely, disciplinary action may be taken by bringing this document to the governing officials.

After completing the document, the governor placed his seal on it. Others, who worked in the government offices under him, signed as official witnesses. It looked like the line of the Great Dipper stretched out vertically, with the three stars lined up at front, when the witnesses were placing their seals.

When the finalized document was read to the rich man in its entirety, his face was confused and he asked,

"That's all it takes to become a *yangban*? I thought that *yangbans* were like immortal figures with supernatural powers. But if that's all there is, my fortune has been wasted. Can't you fix it so that it's more favorable for me?"

Upon hearing the sullen complaints, the governor decided to add a few more points to the document. In the revised document, the following was added:

When people were made by the heavens, they were divided into four groups. Of the four groups, the head is those who were able read ancient texts. These people were distinguished as yangbans.

There are more than just a few advantages to being a yangban, who do not plow the fields or trade in the markets.

He can pass the government entrance exams to become a governing official, only if he is prudent with his studies. Once he takes the seat of office, he can use the wealth and prosperity of the high position, to live in splendor. And if one does not pass the government entrance exam, there is another preparatory exam the Jinsa-si he can take to fully use the rights of a yangban.

With the successful completion of the government entrance

exam, he receives the medallion of successful completion that is only 60cm long, but the honors include various luxuries and rights that others can't buy. He can say that it has full monetary value. Also, once you've entered the government service, no matter how late you entered, you may be placed in high positions—even governing a whole district depending on the status of the family ancestors and their seats in society.

Wherever yangbans go, they are cared for by many servants who carry parasols, with which they keep the skin below the ears white without a trace of a tan. Their waists are well rounded, for their stomach are well fed on the respect of servants. In their private chambers, beautiful women await them, and in the field, full of grain, cranes sing a beautiful melody for them.

Any yangban is free to do whatever he pleases, even if they don't take part in government, or live poorly in the countryside. He could take his neighbors' cow to plow his fields, if he has no cow. He can gather the men to do his work, who would be willing to work for him. If the servants don't listen to him, there is no one to magistrate him if he throws lye on them and pulls their topknots of hair.

The rich man suddenly stood up when the governor wrote this much. His face turned red, and he shook his head as he said,

"Oh, for heaven's sake, stop right there, dear *yangban*, sir! Just forget it! This is ridiculous. Are you going to make me a thief under the heavens and on the earth?"

At that, he went away with the speed of wind, and never again, until his death, did he think of becoming a *yangban*.

Was it possible to
buy and sell one's social status?

Originally, within the caste system, a person's status was defined before birth and was not changeable once it was set. However, in the later part of the Joseon Dynasty, the treasury of the country became empty as it went through several wars, including a war with Japan and a war with China. As the country struggled to sustain itself, the foundation for the *yangban* class also took a hit. At the same time, the agricultural technique was progressing and the market economy was being developed. The new developing class of rich farmers and merchants desired to obtain a higher social status. This led to the trade of the *yangban* birthright between those *yangbans* who desperately needed money and rich citizens who sought a high status. Simply put, it was the buying and selling of the *yangban* status.

The government was aware of this trend but turned a blind eye in order to revive the national economy that became poor due to wars. In the late seventeenth century, the government even made it legal for people to buy and sell official statuses. The policy was called *gong-myung-chup,* which literally means 'a blank appointment paper.' A government official had the power to write in the name of the person on this appointment paper on the spot to anyone who donated money or grains. In this way, a rich citizen could obtain the status as a *yangban* and be eligible for a government position. Though it was a government position in name only, once a person became a *yangban*, he or she was a genuine *yangban* nonetheless. Slowly, the number of *yangbans* grew and the number of the middle class or common class began to decline. This began to shake the caste system to the core. However, it was not until 1894 when the caste system was officially destroyed.

The Story of Heo-Saeng

This literary piece also ridicules the problem of the *yangban* system in those days as *The Story of Yangban* did.

Heo-Saeng, a poor *seonbi*, developed his business skills to build up wealth and used that wealth to look after poor citizens. Contrary to the incapable *yangban* character in *The Story of Yangban*, *yangban* Heo-Saeng was the person responsible for the business of commerce. The author Park Ji-Won stressed the role of commerce and industry, which *yangbans* looked down on as lowly commoner's work, as being the center of the economic renewal and the development of an abundant society.

With ten thousand *nyangs* an old Korean monetary unit, Heo-Saeng bought fruits and the hair of horse tails, which brought the nation into economic suffering. By showing how one man's purchases can dramatically change the market of the entire nation, Heo-Saeng desired to demonstrate how weak the economic system was.

Also, the *yangbans* in this story couldn't perform ancestor worship rituals because they lacked fruits and hair nets ^{Hair nets were used so that the noblemen's topknot would not fall in front of their face}. It showed the misguided culture in which the formality is valued more than one's heart. The author Park Ji-Won wanted to speak against the official customs and incapability of the *yangban* class.

The Story of Heo-Saeng not only delivered a disapproval of the economic situation of the nation, but also addressed the strict foreign policy of Joseon in his time. During those years, the Ming Dynasty collapsed and the Qing Dynasty emerged in China. Joseon, which had friendly political relations with the Ming Dynasty, tried to distance itself from Qing Dynasty claiming that it was a nation of barbarians. For practical benefits, Park Ji-Won believed that it would be beneficial for Joseon to develop good political relations with the Qing Dynasty and actively learn whatever was worth learning.

Toward the end of the novel, the author points out the foolishness of the political actions of the nobles of the ruling class, who worried about the country in words alone without any participation. Simply put, he was saying that only when the *yangbans* come to their senses, the general public can emerge out of poverty and gain political power.

Once upon a time, there lived an educated man named Heo-Saeng in Mukjeok Village in Hanyang ^{Seoul}. Mukjeok Village was a place near Mount Namsan where many poor scholars lived, and among them, Heo-Saeng was especially poor. His straw-roofed house was so old that rain seeped through it during the summer, and the cold wind found its way inside and froze up his nose. But Heo-Saeng had no interest in trying to make a living and only loved to read. He barely got by with his wife's sewing.

One day, after a few days with nothing to eat, his wife asked in the most miserable voice,

"You won't ever take the exam for government officials. Why do you keep reading then?"

Heo-Saeng chuckled and replied,

"I still have much more to learn."

"Then, how about you do the work of making things?"

"I've never learned to make things. How can I do it?"

"Then, how about you sell things?"

"How can I sell things when I've no money to buy things in the first place?"

With that answer, his wife became angry and raised her voice.

"You read day and night, and all you've learned from that is to say 'how can I?' You can't make anything. You can't sell things. Well then, can you learn to *steal*?"

Heo-Saeng closed the book he was reading and got up.

"I began reading with ten years in mind, but I have to stop at year seven. This is too bad."

Heo-Saeng got out of the house, although he had no particular purpose. He wandered here and there. But as he had only stayed inside the house to read day and night, how could he have anyone to talk to? He stopped a man walking on the street and asked,

"Who is the richest person in this region?"

"Of course, it is the man with the last name *Byeon*."

Heo-Saeng then went to find Byeon, and with a respectful bow, began to speak.

"I am a man who learns, and I wish to work, for my family is very poor. I hear you are the richest man in Hanyang. Please lend me ten thousand *nyangs*."

Byeon looked at Heo-Saeng for a while, and then answered, "Sure."

Not saying another word, he gave Heo-Saeng the ten thousand *nyangs*. As soon as he received the money, he went home, not even stopping to say thanks.

Byeon's family and guests were dumbfounded because Heo-Saeng looked no more than a beggar. His belt was nearly worn out, with various strands of thread barely hanging on. The bottom of his shoes had a hole in them, his *gat* was crumpled, and his jacket was dirty. From his nose flowed a clear fluid. How could Byeon give such a man ten thousand *nyangs* at his beckoning? Not only that, but the man had simply turned around without even saying thank you. His children asked him,

"Father, do you know that man?"

The rich man shook his head.

"I met him for the first time today."

"How could you give ten thousand *nyangs* to a man you don't know and not even bother to ask his name?"

Byeon told his sons his reasons in detail.

"Those who come to borrow something from others tend to be exaggerating in their actions. They may boast that they are trustworthy. But in their face you'll be able to see some slavery, and they keep repeating something they'd already said. But that man, as shabby as he might look, still boasts of confidence. That tells me he is not ashamed of his poverty. Whatever a man like that wants to do, I think, is no small matter. I thought I might test this man. And why would I want his name when I have not refused him ten thousand *nyangs*?"

Meanwhile, with the ten thousand *nyangs* in hand, Heo-Saeng headed straight for Anseong, not even stopping by his house. Anseong was a city situated along the border of the Gyeonggi and Chungcheong provinces, and was an important city for merchants from the three provinces—Chungcheong, Gyeongsang, and Jeolla.

Heo-Saeng found a place to live, and from the very next day, began buying up dates, chestnuts, persimmons, pears, pomegranates, oranges, and citron fruits. When word got around that a man named Heo-Saeng was buying up fruit at a price better than the current market, merchants began bringing him fruit from all over the place.

Not long after, there was no more fruit to be bought at Anseong, and this began causing a great chaos. With no fruit to be found in the country, people could no longer hold parties or sacrificial rites. When fruit became precious, its price also went up uncontrollably.

Then, Heo-Saeng opened up his warehouse full of fruit and began selling it. Those who had sold their fruit to Heo-Saeng at twice the regular price were now buying them up at ten times what they had paid him. In no time, the ten thousand *nyangs* had become a hundred thousand. However, Heo-Saeng was far

from joyful. With a deep sigh, he lamented,

"The country almost went down with only ten thousand *nyangs*. I see what kind of economic turmoil it is in."

Next time, Heo-Saeng bought such things as swords, weeding hoes, and clothes. He went down to Jeju Island with all those products and re-sold the items. With the money he got, Heo-Saeng began buying up horsehair.

"In a few years, people in the nation will no longer be able to tie their hair in a topknot."

This was because horsehair was used for headbands. Without horsehair, no headbands could be made. And without a headband, no man would be able to tie his hair in a topknot.

In a little while, the price of a headband went up by ten times. Merchants crossed the sea to buy headbands from Heo-Saeng, and Heo-Saeng made an incredible amount of money just by sitting around.

One day, Heo-Saeng was walking along the sea when he found an old rower. He asked him,

"Is there an empty island around here where people might live?"

"Yes there is. Once, I met a storm and was drifted westward. There, I found an empty island. It had all kinds of flowers and fruits growing on it, and roe, deer, and fish were living there, peacefully together."

Heo-Saeng was much delighted and replied,

"If you take me there, we will be able to live together in much wealth."

The rower waited for a day with good wind and took Heo-Saeng to the island. Heo-Saeng went up to the highest point of the island, looked around, and sighed deeply.

"What could I possibly do on this island that is not even a thousand *li*'s long approximately 400km? Its soil is rich and the taste of its water is good though. I could live like a wealthy old man."

The rower, standing next to him, asked,

"This island is empty. There is no one here. Who would you live with?"

"People gather where there is virtue. I only fear there is no virtue. Why would I worry about that when there is no one here?"

At the time, the region of Byeonsan was bursting with thieves. The king had tried to capture them all by releasing an army into the region, but the thieves had only retreated farther into the mountainside. The nation was worried that the thieves might return, and the thieves were beginning to starve because they had been forced into the mountain.

Hearing this, Heo-Saeng went to the leader of the thieves.

"If a thousand of you stole a thousand *nyangs*, how much money would you take each?"

"I guess just a *nyang* each."

"You guys do not have wives?"

"No."

"Do you have land to farm on?"

The leader chuckled and replied, "No. If we had land and family, why would we have become thieves?"

"I see. So you are saying you would no longer be a thief if you had land to farm on and family to raise! Fine! I will see if I can find some money for you. Tomorrow, go out to the sea. There, you'll find a boat with a red flag. The boat will have money in it. Take as much as you need."

The thieves laughed at Heo-Saeng, calling him a lunatic.

But the next day, the thieves went out to the sea and they were surprised to find a boat with a red flag on it. When the thieves saw that there was three hundred thousand *nyangs* inside, they all bowed before Heo-Saeng.

"From now on, we will only obey your words, master."

Heo-Saeng told the thieves, "Here is money. Take as much as you want."

The thieves all found a bag of money and carried it on their backs. But not even the strongest man could carry more than a hundred *nyangs*. At that sight, Heo-Saeng laughed out loud.

"Ha-ha, how are you planning on becoming thieves when you can barely carry a bag of a hundred *nyangs*? You can no longer go back to your hometown even if you wanted to. Your names are all written on the list of thieves. I will wait for you here. Take a hundred *nyangs* each and find a cow to farm your land and a woman to be your wife."

A few days later, every single thief returned with a cow and a woman. Heo-Saeng, meanwhile, had prepared food for two thousand people. Taking the people, the food, and the cows, Heo-Saeng went to the empty island he had found before. Since Heo-Saeng disappeared with the thieves, the nation no longer had to worry about them.

As soon as they arrived on the island, Heo-Saeng and the thieves built houses out of trees and farmed the land. The soil was so rich that the harvest was plentiful every year. They collected enough food to last for three years and sold the rest to the nearby island. The island next to them almost starved to death because they had nothing to eat. But, they earned even more money.

A few years later, Heo-Saeng asked everyone on the island to come together and said,

"When I first brought you to the island, I had thought of teaching you things from the books as well as manners after settling you down. But since the island is small and my virtue not sufficient, I am going to leave. When you have children, teach them to hold their spoons on their right hand and to yield to those who were born even a day earlier than they were."

Heo-Saeng threw fifty thousand *nyangs* in the sea, and asked them to burn and destroy all the ships except the one he was going out on.

"If you do not go to them, they will not come to you either. Do not correspond with other islands. Since learning is the origin of all wraths, anyone who knows a little bit of the books must come with me."

Heo-Saeng came back to the mainland, travelled to all parts of the nation, and gave his money to the poor. And since he still had a hundred thousand *nyangs* left over, he thought he would pay back the money he owed the rich man.

When Heo-Saeng visited Byeon, Byeon was perplexed.

"Why, you don't look too good. You must have lost all ten thousand *nyangs*."

At that remark, Heo-Saeng chuckled and put before him hundred thousand *nyangs*.

"Only people like you speak of becoming healthy at the sight of prosperity. How could ten thousand *nyangs* fatten up one's virtue? Here is your money. I once could not overcome my hunger, stop reading, and had to borrow ten thousand *nyangs* from you. I am embarrassed to have done that."

When Heo-Saeng replied so, Byeon bowed before him and told him he would only take the original amount and the interest accrued on tenth of the ten thousand. However, Heo-Saeng became greatly upset and asked if he was taking him for a mere peddler.

When Heo-Saeng gave him the money and left, Byeon quietly followed him. When he saw Heo-Saeng enter a nearly-destroyed straw-house at the corner of Mount Namsan, Byeon asked an old woman sitting by the well, "That small straw-house, whose is it?"

"That is the house of Heo-Saeng. He refused to let go of his precious books even in the face of poverty. One day, he set out and hasn't been heard from for five years. His wife lives alone and offers a memorial service every year on the day of his disappearance."

The next day, Byeon visited Heo-Saeng's house and offered to give him his money back, but he flat out refused.

"If I desired to be rich, would I have gotten rid of a million *nyangs* and taken ten thousand? Take the money and just send me and my wife some food every once in a while so that we do not starve. Any more than that is a burden for me."

Byeon decided to grant Heo-Saeng's wish. Every once in a while, he took some food and clothes to his house and left it there. Heo-Saeng gladly took Byeon's help, but whenever he brought him more than he needed, he did not seem pleased.

Sometimes, Byeon took with him a bottle of alcohol and the

two talked through the night. Several years passed and the two became close friends.

One day, after a few drinks, Byeon asked Heo-Saeng,

"How in the world were you able to collect a million *nyangs* in five years?"

"It was easy. Our nation does not trade with other countries, nor does it even do business within its regions. Everything is produced and spent within one region. When someone takes with him a lot of money and buys up one thing from the region, would its price not go up? It's therefore very easy to earn a lot of money. But such a tactic can also bring the people to poverty and eventually bring down the whole nation."

Byeon found it unfortunate that such an intelligent man as Heo-Saeng was living in a remote place. So he mentioned Heo-Saeng to General Yi Wan The original title is *Eoyeong Daejang*, used to refer to the head of *Eoyeong Cheong*, a capital branch of the Joseon military system, who he knew well. The general very much wanted to meet Heo-Saeng.

One day, Byeon went to Heo-Saeng's house with the general. However, Heo-Saeng refused to even acknowledge the general. After only focusing on his drinking for the better part of the night, he asked the general, "What is the reason you have come to visit me at this hour?"

When the general mentioned that the nation was looking for wise men, Heo-Saeng said it was boring and lifted his hands in protest. Then he asked, "What is your position?"

"I am a general."

"Then you're pretty high up in the government. Well, I am able to recommend to you a man who is like the character Jegal Gongmyeong ^{Zhuge Liang} in *Samgukji*. The Record of Three Kingdoms. It is a book that tells the history of the three nations of what is now China. Zhuge Liang was a character in *Samgukji*, well known as a man for whom the king himself went into his straw-house three times. But in order for you to get the man, the king himself has to go to him three times. Think he's up for that?"

The general shook his head. "That is going to be difficult to do. Do you have a better idea?"

"The Ming Dynasty is almost completely destroyed. The generals and their soldiers have fled their country. They are now in our nation and living a life of wanderers. They are demanding that we return the favour they showed us during *Imjin Waeran* ^{a war} between Japan and Korea in 1592–1598. Could you ask the royal court to marry the daughters of the king and the aristocrats to them and pass their houses over to them?"

The general lowered his head and pondered for a good while.

"That is not going to be possible, either."

"If you say 'this is not possible' and 'that's not possible,' then what can you do? Well then, there is a very easy task you can carry out. Do you think you're up for it?"

"Well, tell me."

Heo-Saeng went on. "In order to capture the tiger, one has to enter its cave. And in order to complete a great task, one first has to become familiar with heroes from all over. It is difficult to successfully invade another country without sending a spy to that land first. The Qing Dynasty is currently occupying the land of China. So we must establish a relation with them so that we are able to freely cross their border. Send the children of officials to the Qing Empire, and have them befriend the talents of Qing. Also, have merchants freely come and go. They will be glad that Joseon is befriending them.

Have sons of *yangban* wear Qing clothes, give them Qing style haircuts, and send them to Qing. Have them work for the government, befriend figures from that area, and find out about the conditions of that country. Then our country will turn the whole world upside down and will we not cleanse ourselves of our shame?"

General Yi Wan listened to Heo-Saeng and with a deep sigh, replied, "That might sound like a good idea, but who among the high class would send their precious child to that savage country? And we take pride in our manners; we value it more than our own lives. Who would be willing to cut their hair into a pigtail and wear Chinese clothing?"

At that, Heo-Saeng became greatly upset and screamed.

"What are these so-called 'aristrocrats' doing? They say 'manners, manners,' but do they even know what manners are? They wish to punish their nation, but they're not willing to strip themselves of their hairbands and their troublesome clothes? We need to ride horses, shoot arrows, and throw spears. But they're not willing to cut their broad sleeves because of 'manners'?"

Then, Heo-Saeng fixed his eyes on the general.

"It is the same thing with you! I have already given you three options, but you shake your head and say you can't carry out any of it. You're a hopeless man! How could you call yourself a trustworthy servant? We must begin by cutting the heads of men like you!"

Then, Heo-Saeng got up, searched for a sword, and tried to stab General Yi with it. Shocked out of his mind, the general ran away through the back door.

The next morning, General Yi went back to Heo-Saeng's house. However, he found that the house was empty. Heo-Saeng was nowhere to be seen.

Who were *seonbis*?

Seonbi is a word to describe an honorable person with knowledge. It referred to a member of a ruling class in the society who had the eligibility to become a government administrator. When someone was described as *seonbi*-like, it commonly meant he or she was like a Confucian scholar of moral honesty and integrity. *Seonbis* insisted on having right values and walked the right path with single-mindedness.

Of course, not all *seonbis* lived the life of moral honesty. There were many who, like those represented in *The Story of Yangban and The Story of Heo-Saeng*, were unskillful in doing things other than reading books. For this reason, the positive image of a *seonbi* as an upright and straight person was connected with the negative image of a stuffy person lacking flexibility and common sense.

Yangbans including *seonbis* wore a robe called "*dopo*" and a hat called "*gat*" on the head. Inside the *gat*, hair was tied with a topknot and banded with a headband called "*mang-geon*" to prevent it from flowing down the face.

Costume of Seonbi

Gat

Mang-geon

Dopo

Hong Gil-Dong Jeon
The Story of Hong Gil-Dong

The Story of Hong Gil-Dong was the first novel written in the Korean alphabet by Heo Gyun (1569–1618) during the Joseon Dynasty. This story, still very popular to this day, often reappears in the form of cartoons and children's stories.

The Story of Hong Gil-Dong exposes many public problems of those days. The society represented in the story, not only has the problem of differential treatment between *yangbans* and citizens, but also the problem of differential treatment between a legitimate son and an illegitimate son. A *yangban* man could have, besides his lawful wife, several mistresses. However, a son born to a mistress, called a *seoja* ^{illegitimate son}, was treated differently than a son born to the lawful wife, a *jeokja* ^{legitimate son}. This difference came into play especially when inheritance was divided or when ancestor worship ceremonies were performed that required *jeokja* to represent the household. More painfully, a *seoja* was prohibited from addressing his father as 'father' and his brother as 'brother'. Furthermore, a *seoja* was lawfully banned from taking the government entrance examination and he could not go into the path of a government official regardless of his talents.

Heo Gyun, who was a *jeoka* himself, became interested in the troubles of *seojas* because of his teacher Yi Dal. Yi Dal was a famous poet in his time, but due to the limitations of his status as a *seoja*, spent his life in booze and wandering.

Being born into a rich family, Heo Gyun passed the government entrance exam in 1594. He held several positions in the government, but he never liked the life of an official due to his free-spirited nature. He showed interests in the marginalized and was critical of society. He was charged of betrayal and was executed in 1618.

In the world of *The Story of Hong Gil-Dong*, we find corrupt officials who fed their stomachs with the taxes paid by the people as well as poor citizens, who had no other option than taking the path of robbery out of hunger and poverty. At the end of this story, Hong Gil-Dong establishes the nation of Yuldo and becomes its king, which shows the author's intention to eradicate corruption in the society and build a utopia.

Once upon a time, during the reign of King Sejong of Joseon (1397–1450), there was a minister with the last name Hong. He was from a family with distinguished ancestry. As a young man, he passed the government entrance examination and reached the position of Minister of Personnel.

One day, Minister Hong dreamt a strange dream while taking a nap in the reception room. Out of nowhere, thunder and lightning shook the sky. A blue dragon appeared and rushed fiercely toward Minister Hong and entered his mouth. He became startled and woke up from his dream. "This is a dream of the forthcoming conception of a baby. Surely, I will have a precious son."

Thinking about the dream, Minister Hong entered the inner chamber of the house and looked for his wife. However, his wife did not like the idea of sleeping with him in the broad daylight.

In that moment, a maidservant named Chun-Some brought in tea. Minister Hong slept with Chun-Some instead. Though she was a slave, eighteen year-old Chun-Some was a pretty and virtuous woman. Ten months from that day, Chun-Some gave birth to a handsome son. Minister Hong named him Gil-Dong.

Gil-Dong grew rapidly. He was also wise and smart enough to learn one hundred things when taught only one lesson. Moreover, he was big in height and very strong. Minister Hong cherished the boy and gave him a portion of fine food and silk whenever he had the chance. However, there always was a shadow cast on his face. He thought, "What good is it to eat fine food and wear smooth silk? I cannot even call my father 'father' and my brother 'brother.'"

During those days, there was great discrimination against *seojas*. ^{illegitimate children} Since *seojas* were not recognized as legitimate sons, they had to address their fathers as 'master.' Furthermore, they had to call their half-brothers, born to the

lawful wives of their fathers as 'young master.' Also, it did not matter how much they studied or improved their military skills, they could not even apply to take the government test or obtain a position in the government. Gil-Dong knew very well about these facts of life, so his heart was always heavy.

One autumn night, Minister Hong saw Gil-Dong taking a stroll in the back yard. Gil-Dong did this in order to bring peace to his troubled heart.

Minister Hong asked, "How come you cannot sleep in this late night?"

"I heard that men are the most precious among all the creatures created by heaven. How is it that I, born as a human being, am not treated well? How can I call myself a human being?"

Pretending to be clueless, Minister Hong asked, "What are you talking about?"

"Since I cannot call my father 'father' and my brother 'brother,' how can I say that I am a human being? Even the young servants look down on me. I feel angry and mistreated."

Overwhelmed by his sadness, Gil-Dong broke into tears. Seeing this, Minister Hong felt pain in his heart.

Not wanting to weaken his spirit by comforting him in vain, Minister Hong raised his voice in rebuke.

"Are you the only one born as a *seoja* in this world? How is it that you make such a big deal out of it? If you shed tears again in regards to this matter, I will surely not forgive you."

Upon returning to his room, Gil-Dong bawled alone trying to alleviate his sadness.

In the morning, Gil-Dong went over to his mother's room and said,

"Your son, being born a man, dreams of doing great things. However, due to my lowly status, it is hard to make that dream into reality. If possible, I would like to leave this house and see the big world. Mother, forgive me for not serving you in devotion by being next to you. Please forget about this ungrateful son of yours and live healthily unto your old age."

Gil-Dong bowed to his mother and walked out of the house.

He walked wherever his path led.

For many days, he walked. Gil-Dong found himself walking

into deep woods where there were densely packed trees and where the water was clear. Searching for a house with people, his path led to a big town that had several hundred houses in a wide open area. There was some kind of banquet going on and people were gathered in one place eating and drinking.

It was obviously that this was where a band of thieves lived. The thieves were in the process of electing their leader.

Thinking that he should stay in this place, Gil-Dong strode ahead to where the people were.

"My name is Hong Gil-Dong and I am a *seoja* of Minister Hong in Hanyang. After leaving my house, I was searching for a place to live and I came this far. Since heaven led me here, how about if I become your leader?"

At first, all the thieves laughed at him. But when they saw Gil-Dong lifting and moving a rock as huge as a house and uprooting a huge tree from the ground, they bowed before him.

"No one among us was able to move that rock. You are indeed a man of great strength. From now on, be our leader and lead us."

Gil-Dong and the thieves pledged as brothers of lifelong unity and solidarity by shedding the blood of a white horse.

Gil-Dong and the thieves struck the storehouse of Haein-sa

Buddhist Temple in Hapcheon.

Using a strategy to avoid a big confrontation, they were able to steal the food and precious possessions that filled the storehouse.

From this point on, Gil-Dong named his band of thieves "Hwalbin-Dang," meaning "the group that saves poor people." Taking his band of thieves all across the land, Gil-Dong punished corrupt officials bent on harassing people and stole their wealth, only to distribute it to the poor.

Since he decided to become the leader of thieves, Gil-Dong wanted to leave a great legacy behind. One day, he weaved hay into seven scarecrows. Laying scarecrows on the ground, he recited a spell, bringing them to life in the exact appearance of Gil-Dong himself. All his servants were so stunned to witness this scene.

Being eight in number including himself, Gil-Dong divided the thieves into groups of fifty and assigned each "Gil-Dong" a company of these fifty men. Then, he scattered them all over the land.

These groups robbed the storehouses of all those who stole their wealth through illegal means and distributed them to the poor. This made all the corrupt magistrates and rich people greatly insecure that they were unable to sleep well at night. However, the public praised and thanked Gil-Dong.

The officials all over the country decided to bring a petition to the king in Hanyang.

"Majesty, the thief named Hong Gil-Dong is robbing each town's treasury. Even the transports of goods on the way to Hanyang from each province are being interrupted in the middle. If we allow this to keep happening, then surely it will be to your loss as well. We beseech you to issue a command to arrest this pack of thieves."

The funny thing was that something like this was happening not only in one place but all over the land at the same time. All the provinces, Pyeongan, Chungcheong, Gyeongsang, Jeolla, Gangwon, and Gyeonggi, reported that it was Hong Gil-Dong who had

done this.

The king commanded the police bureau to bring Hong Gil-Dong in. However, even the police force, including its captain, kept on being embarrassed by Hong Gil-Dong and Hwalbin-Dang, and failed to take them into custody. The actions of Gil-Dong became bolder by the day. It reached a point where there was no one in the country that had not heard of his name.

The king became greatly dismayed by this.

"It is a pity that all the masters of martial arts cannot catch a simple thief like him..."

Seeing the king like this, one of his men told him, "Majesty, Hong Gil-Dong is an illegitimate son of the former Minister of Personnel, Minister Hong. He is also a brother of Hong Gil-Hyun, who is the deputy minister of defense. If you bring his father and brother into custody, Hong Gil-Dong cannot help but walk in here."

"That's a great idea."

The king immediately placed Minister Hong under arrest at the department of justice. The king also bestowed the governorship of Gyeongsang Province to Hong Gil-Hyun and commanded him to catch his brother, Gil-Dong, within one year.

At once, Gil-Hyun took his place as the governor of Gyeongsang

Province and placed the following notice on every intersection of every town.

To my younger brother Gil-Dong,

Because of you, our father, who is over eighty years of age, has been placed under arrest and become ill while in imprisonment. Even the king has become so worried because of you. Where in the world can anyone find this kind of unfaithfulness by a son and disobedience by a citizen? I beseech you to return on your own and help bring our father back to health and help this country rid of worries.

Your brother, Hong Gil-Hyun

After posting this notice, Gil-Hyun looked after the health of his father and waited for Gil-Dong to appear. Then, one day, a young man came looking for Gil-Hyun. As soon as he entered, he bowed to Gil-Hyun and cried, "My older brother! I committed a grievous sin. Please have me killed."

That young man was Gil-Dong himself. After telling his servants off, Gil-Hyun held Gil-Dong's hand and cried bitterly saying, "How long has it been? Though we meet for the first time in a long time, I cannot help but feel sad. How is it that you use your talents and wisdom to cause chaos for the country? Since the law of the land is strict, what shall I do?"

"I came here today in order to ease the family's worry. When the dawn breaks, please put me in chains and transport me to Hanyang."

The following morning, Gil-Dong was transported to Hanyang. Strangely, however, it was not one Gil-Dong that was brought to Hanyang but eight. Eight Gil-Dongs argued among themselves, claiming that each was the real Gil-Dong.

Not knowing what to do, the king brought out Minister Hong and said, "The only one who can tell which is the real son is the father himself. Now, show me which of these Gil-Dongs is the real one."

Shedding tears, Minister Hong pled with eight Gil-Dongs. "My dear Gil-Dong, how is it that you mistreat me by playing this trick. Why don't you come forth and bear punishment that the king is about to dispense?"

In response to Minister Hong's rebuke, eight Gil-Dongs bowed their heads in unison and said,

"Having been born of a lowly slave, I could not address my

154

father 'father' and my brother 'brother.' That became a sore spot for me and I had to leave my family behind. I wandered around aimlessly until I joined a pack of thieves. However, I never touched the possessions of innocent people; but instead, I robbed the possessions of unjust people and wealth of those who received bribes."

Hearing this, the king became enraged and said, "Didn't you trick the monks of the temple Haein-sa in Hapcheon and steal their possessions? Isn't that a sin?"

"Originally, Buddhism was all about becoming a Buddha through the way of self-discipline. But today, they focus only on cheating people and robbing their possessions. They take food from people, but they themselves do not farm. They take clothes from people, but they themselves do not make clothes. What are they if not true thieves? Now, if you are enraged like this, it would be better for me to die."

Finished speaking, eight Gil-Dongs fell forward all at once and turned into scarecrows. The king became all the more enraged and issued a command to arrest Hong Gil-Dong immediately. But Gil-Dong could not be arrested.

Then, one day, the following notice was posted in various places.

I, Hong Gil-Dong, wished to become the minister of defense all my life.

If the king were to generously bestow this position unto me, then I will voluntarily appear.

The king's men told the king,

"Majesty, after posting a false notice saying that you would make his wish come true, it would be strategic to arrest him when he appears."

The king posted the notice saying that he would grant Gil-Dong's wish to become the minister of defense.

After a little while, Gil-Dong reappeared in the robe of the minister of defense and bowed before the king.

"Having been born of a lowly slave, I never thought I would ever obtain a position in the government. Due to your grace, Majesty, I am given the position of the minister of defense. For this, I am truly grateful."

The king came down from his throne and handed the appointment papers to Gil-Dong in person.

"As you wish, I bestow unto you the title of the minister of defense. Now, please oversee the military of this country and maintain national security well."

"I am forever grateful to you, Majesty."

For a long time, Gil-Dong gazed at the appointment papers and shed tears. Then, he hopped onto a cloud and disappeared.

After that, the country was peaceful for a very long time. No longer did magistrates receive bribes, and the Manchurian barbarians that used to come over the border and go on rampages completely disappeared. The king believed that it was all due to the work of Hong Gil-Dong, the minister of defense.

Meanwhile, Gil-Dong had left Joseon and went around the world. However, upon finding an island suitable for habitation by people, he returned to the pack of Hwalbin-Dang and said,

"On the date that I point out, go and prepare a ship and wait for me on the riverbank. I will go and prepare three thousand sacks of rice for us and return. Let us all move to that island and live there. Do not ever forget that promised date."

On the promised day, Gil-Dong and his comrades moved to the island with three thousand sacks of rice. Upon arriving at the island, they built houses and plowed the land on which they would farm. Those that did not want to be farmers became merchants. Everyone worked happily and diligently in their given role.

Though the island was small, each town was able to produce unique products. Gil-Dong had people turn in their goods. By selling the goods overseas for high prices, Gil-Dong was able to make profits which he returned to the people. The lifestyle of the people became better by the day. Gil-Dong also manufactured weapons and recruited soldiers to be trained in martial arts.

Much time had passed, and Minister Hong died in his nineties. Before his death, Minister Hong asked his oldest son, Gil-Hyun, to look after Gil-Dong and his mother. Learning of the forthcoming death of his father, Gil-Dong tried to return home in a hurry. However, he missed being with his father in his last hour. Gil-Dong put on a lavish funeral for his father and prepared his grave in the best place in the island. Next to his father's grave, Gil-Dong lived for the next three years, since there was a tradition of building a hut near the parents' tomb and living there for three years, singing songs of grief at every meal time.

When he had finished the requirement of tending to his father's grave for three years, Gil-Dong gathered his servants and said, "Until when are we going to live contently in this small island? There is a country nearby with the name of Yuldo. Let us overrun it."

The land of the kingdom of Yuldo was fertile, surrounded by the sea, and people there lived in luxury. Because there was not a country nearby, it was a perfect target for the attack.

Choosing a good day for the attack, Gil-Dong led his army into the kingdom of Yuldo. The king of Yuldo fought against them, but soon the forces of Yuldo were defeated and the king surrendered. Once inside the castle, Gil-Dong calmed the people of Yuldo down and hosted a great banquet, thereby earning their good will.

Finally, Gil-Dong became the king of Yuldo. Not only the servants of Gil-Dong, but also the people of the kingdom of Yuldo cried, "Hurray!" and welcomed their new king. Upon his ascension to the throne, the kingdom of Yuldo became all the more peaceful and the people lived in peace and happiness. The Manchurian barbarians did not even think about crossing the border.

In this way, Gil-Dong enjoyed his long reign with his people. Gil-Dong passed away thirty years after his ascension to the throne.

Was Hong Gil-Dong a real person?

It seems that *The Story of Hong Gil-Dong* was written based on historical facts. In *The Chronicles of the Joseon Dynasty*, the name Gil-Dong, appears frequently. It is not known what kind of thief he was, what kind of punishment he received, or how he died. However, it is clear that he was a well-known figure whose notoriety kept an age spellbound. This leads us to believe that Heo Gyun might have heard about this well-known thief and created a fictitious character out of this historical Gil-Dong. The fact that he was a thief, that he terrorized government officials, and that he received support of some people in the society were also characteristics of the main character in the novel.

The Story of Hong Gil-Dong, which was originally written either in late sixteenth century or early seventeenth century, is said to have drawn great popularity in late nineteenth century and early twentieth century. It was the same time period in which the power of the central government could not reach the rural areas, just as the Joseon Dynasty had declined. Furthermore, with the invasion of foreign powers such as the Japanese, the people of Korea had a very difficult time to go on living.

During this time, many took Hong Gil-Dong as their role model and organized themselves into a real-life Hwalbin-Dang. These people imitated Hong Gil-Dong by giving advance notices before attacking and stealing from municipal courts, Buddhist temples, and the rich. They also distributed these goods to the poor. The fact that *The Story of Hong Gil-Dong* was widely read in those days, perhaps points to the people's longing for the emergence of a hero who could help the commoners.

Parkssi Buin Jeon

The Story of Lady Park

The Story of Lady Park is a representative classical novel written during the later part of the Joseon Dynasty. It is a story of a woman with the last name Park, who courageously protected her family and rescued her country. If Hong Gil-Dong was a hero who fought societal corruptions, Lady Park was a heroine who rescued the country from a great danger.

The context of the novel is set in the time of the Manchu War of 1636. This war was started by the invasion of Qing China in 1636 during the reign of King Injo (1595–1649) of Joseon. Korea lost the war and King Injo suffered the humiliation of surrender in Samjeon Island. In that event, King Injo had to perform the dishonorable ritual of surrender in prostrating before the Qing emperor three times and bowing nine times. After this, the crown prince, other princes, and those high ranking officials who opposed surrender were taken as captives to Qing China. Without a question, the remaining people had to endure great suffering.

For the king of our country to bow his head to a king of another country, especially the king of the country that Koreans viewed as barbaric, was an event that deeply hurt the pride of the Korean people. People wished, "Only if someone could lead Joseon to victory". This novel emerged out of that wish. Within the ficticious world of a novel, Lady Park forces a Qing general to kneel and also cuts off the head of his brother. In this way, the novel became a means of bringing comfort to the hearts of the people that were saddened by the war.

Then, why was it that heroine Park, who helped people voice their anger, had to be a woman? The men in *The Story of Lady Park*, on the contrary, are portrayed as stubborn people who ultimately bring their country to ruins by ignoring Lady Park's advice. This marks the desire of women who found themselves burdened by life and wanted to be free, at least in the world of fiction. Furthermore, this is a criticism and ridicule of the men who failed to carry out the task of defending their country.

During the reign of King Injo of Joseon, there lived a man named Yi Deuk-Chun. He started his career as a government official as a young man and served his country loyally. Also, he was virtuous and humble and he ruled over people justly. There was no one in the country that did not know his name. People, while praising him, envied his wealth and fame too.

He had a son named Shi-Baek. Shi-Baek was so bright and intelligent that when given one lesson, he would understand a hundred things. Yi Deuk-Chun and his wife, Lady Kang, were greatly proud of their son.

Much time had passed and Shi-Baek reached the age of sixteen. Mr. and Mrs. Yi decided to find a wise and beautiful young woman who would be compatible with their son and have them bound in marriage.

One day, as Yi Deuk-Chun was sitting and playing a flute in the garden, a *seonbi* named Chu-sa Park <small>Chu-Sa refers to a *seonbi* that lives in nature without working for the government</small> came to visit him. Chu-sa Park and Yi Deuk-Chun played flutes and games of chess together for many days. Chu-sa Park proposed that his daughter and Deuk-Chun's son, Shi-Baek, get married. Realizing right away that Park was not any ordinary man, Yi Deuk-Chun agreed to the proposal and showed him great hospitality.

Finally, the day of wedding arrived. Yi Deuk-Chun and his son went to Mount Geumgang and brought the bride home. Seeing the bride for the first time under a bright light, Yi Deuk-Chun and Shi-Baek were startled. The bride's face was awfully ugly. She had gigantic eyes and a protruding forehead. Her facial complexion was dark and her skin was as rough as the bark of a tree. She was also as tall as a totem pole and her waist was as thick as a tree trunk. She gave off a body odour that was appalling.

After calming himself down, Yi Deuk-Chun said to his son,

"Now that I have seen her, she seems worthy and I believe that she would bring many blessings to our family."

Shi-Baek was not about to oppose his father's wish, but he almost fainted thinking about spending his lifetime with an unsightly woman like her.

Even after saying the marital bow, Shi-Baek did not go into the marital chamber to be with his bride. Whenever he was rebuked by his father, he forced himself to go into the room. But upon seeing his bride's face, he would run out again.

His mother, Lady Kang, was frequently mean to the bride for eating too much. Because of this, even the servants began to mistreat her.

Lady Park, then, went to her father-in-law and asked him to build a small cottage for her. She stayed there all by herself only accompanied by her maidservant, Gye-Hwa. She named the cottage Pihwa-Dang, meaning "the refuge away from harm." Lady Park built a garden around the cottage in which she planted all kinds of fragrant plants and spent time taking care of them.

One day, Lady Park told her father-in-law, Yi Deuk-Chun,
"Father, send one of the servants to the horse market tomorrow morning. Out of the tens of thousands of horses there, make

him buy the ugliest one with bare spots on its worn-out skin. When he asks for the price, the seller will say, "Seven *nyangs*." However, have him buy it for three hundred *nyangs* instead and bring it home."

Yi Deuk-Chun was greatly perplexed and asked, "Why? Why pay three hundred *nyangs* when the price for the horse is only seven *nyangs*?"

"You will know the reason later. But please do as I ask."

Sensing that his daughter-in-law had a special ability, Yi Deuk-Chun agreed to do as she proposed.

Receiving the order of Yi Deuk-Chun, the servant went to the horse market the next day. Just like what the master said, the servant found a horse that fit the description.

When asked about the price of the horse, the merchant said, "There are so many fine horses here. Why do you want to buy that skinny one? Pay seven *nyangs* and take it away."

"My master told me to buy it for three hundred *nyangs*. So, take the money."

The horse merchant's eyes got huge. He asked, "What do you mean? Why do you pay three hundred *nyangs* when the price is only seven *nyangs*?"

"I don't know. I am just following my master's order."

"Well, it is fine with me to make a lot of money. But this is way too much... Let's do this instead. Why don't we take seven *nyangs* out and divide the rest between us? You can just tell your master that you paid all three hundred *nyangs*, can't you?"

Convinced by what the merchant said, the servant did accordingly and brought the horse home.

Lady Park closely inspected the horse for a while and told her father-in-law,

"Tell the servant to take the horse back."

"We paid three hundred *nyangs* for this horse. Why do you say we should take it back?"

"The horse is worth three hundred *nyangs*. But since we paid a lot less, what good is it? If you want, you can ask the servant."

The servant was taken aback to hear this and confessed what he did and asked for forgiveness. Then, he went back to the merchant, paid the full three hundred *nyangs*, and returned.

Having been satisfied, Lady Park smiled contently and shared a recipe for raising the horse.

"This horse should eat the porridge of one *doe* ^{approximately 1.8 L} of sesame seeds and five *hops* ^{1 *hop* = 1/10 of 1 *doe*} of white rice a day. Every night, the horse needs to be set free in the yard and covered by cold morning dew. In three years, there will be an opportunity

168

when we can put it to good use."

Yi Deuk-Chun followed through with her daughter-in-law's instructions.

Before they knew it, three years passed. After saying morning greetings to her father-in-law, Lady Park told him, "Tomorrow, a delegation will come from Ming China. The ambassador will most definitely come through the South Gate. Send a trustworthy servant with the horse and make him stand there. The ambassador will covet the horse and ask for its price. Have the servant tell him that the price is thirty thousand *nyangs*. Then, the ambassador will pay the full price and buy it."

The following morning, Yi Deuk-Chun ordered a servant to take the horse out to the South Gate. It was not even noon that the servant returned with thirty thousand *nyangs*, the price of the horse. Shocked, Yi Deuk-Chun asked his daughter-in-law to explain.

"That horse can run a thousand *li* approximately 400 km a day. Since the land of Joseon is so small, there is neither a need for the horse nor anyone who recognizes its value. However, China is a big country and the ambassador was bound to recognize the horse's true value and willing to pay a great sum of money for it."

Yi Deuk-Chun could not help but be amazed by his daughter-in-law's remarkable ability. During that time, Yi Shi-Baek, Lady Park's husband, was studying to pass the government entrance test.

This test was to appoint the bright and talented people to various positions in the government.

The night before the test, Lady Park had a dream. There were flowers in bloom in the pond of Pihwa-Dang with bees and butterflies flying over it. Also, there was a white bowl floating about in the water. This kind of bowl was usually used for holding water for writing calligraphy. Suddenly, this bowl turned into a blue dragon and soared up to heaven in the beautiful clouds.

Immediately after waking up, Lady Park went outside. Just like her dream, there was a white bowl on the edge of the pond! Lady Park had her maidservant take the bowl and give it to Shi-Baek.

"My lady said that if you use this bowl when taking the test today, you will have good news later on."

Sure enough, Shi-Baek took the top spot among all those who passed the test. Even the king took delight in Shi-Baek and

commended him to become the leader of the nation. A banquet was hosted to congratulate this happy occasion. However, because of her unsightly face, she could not be in front of people and stayed behind the scenes.

Soon, it had been five years since Lady Park married into the Yi family. One night when the moonlight was bright and a cool breeze blew in, there was a sound of a crane crying from afar and a cloud with Chu-sa Park of Mount Geumgang on board descended onto the ground. Yi Deuk-Chun hurried down to the yard and greeted Park.

"The reason that I came is to help my daughter rid of her disability. Until now, my daughter has been living with the ugly mask on due to her many sins in her previous reincarnation. Fortunately, that karma came to an end and so does her disability."

Then, Park went over to his daughter's chamber and told her about how to fix her disability. That night, Lady Park got rid of her ugly appearance and transformed herself into a beautiful woman like no other. Everyone in the household, including Yi Deuk-Chun, was so shocked.

Among them, the most surprised was Shi-Baek himself. Though he wanted to run to her right away, he could not do so, thinking about how insensitive and neglectful he had been toward her.

"Since I mistreated her based on her appearance, how can I see her face now? How foolish I have been!"

Shi-Baek greatly regretted having judged his wife based on her appearance instead of her good heart and abilities. Shi-Baek asked for his wife's forgiveness and he loved her deeply and he never made her feel alone again.

During those days, the Ming Dynasty had collapsed and the Qing Dynasty built by the Manchurian tribes, took over in China. The emperor of Qing China wanted to extend the reputation of his nation by attacking Joseon and forcing its surrender. However, because he knew there were great men in Joseon such as Yi Shi-Baek and General Im Gyung-Up, he could not make light of Joseon.

The empress of Qing China tried to assassinate Yi Shi-Baek and General Im Gyung-Up by sending a woman named Gi Hong-Dae, who excelled in resourcefulness, courage, and beauty. After training Gi Hong-Dae in the Joseon language, culture, and manners, the empress bestowed a sword and said, "Go and kill Yi Shi-Baek of Hanyang first. On your way back, go and kill Im Gyung-Up who is guarding the border in Uiju. If you come back having achieved success, then I will reward you greatly."

Lady Park intuitively felt that danger was approaching from Qing China and said to her husband,

"My dear husband, please take note of my words. Tomorrow after sunset, a *gisaeng* from Wonju of Gangwon Province named Seol Jung-Mae will come to visit you. If you fall prey to her beauty and ruse by keeping her close, then you will see great harm. However, if you talk her into coming and seeing me, then I will take care of it."

Not taking her seriously, Shi-Baek told her that he would do as advised.

The sun had set the next day and Yi Shi-Baek was reading books in the room. A certain woman opened the door and came in quietly into the room and bowed to him modestly. She said, "I am a *gisaeng* named Seol Jung-Mae and I live in Wonju. From afar, I heard of your fame and longed for you for a long time. I came here to serve you tonight and I beg you to take delight in me."

The voice of the woman was as fair as the sound of jade beads rolling on a tray and her appearance was as beautiful as a flower.

Though Shi-Baek wavered a little due to her beauty, he remembered Lady Park's words of the previous night and tried to calm himself down.

"It is admirable that you came a long way to see me. However, this is a place frequented by guests from outside. Go to Lady Park's chamber in the backyard. When the night is deepened and guests go back home, then I will call you quietly."

Putting her guard down, the woman went to see Lady Park. With a gentle smile, Lady Park welcomed Seol Jung-Mae and told her maidservant, Gye-Hwa, to bring in wine and snacks. After drinking much per Lady Park's insistence, Seol Jung-Mae's mind became fuzzy and she fell into a deep sleep. In the meantime, Lady Park found a dagger hidden inside Seol Jung-Mae's clothes. However, when Lady Park tried to pull out the dagger, it suddenly began to move as if it were dancing and leaping towards her. As she instinctively moved away from the tip of the blade, she recited a chant. Then, the dagger lost all movement and fell to the ground immediately.

The following morning, when Seol Jung-Mae woke up from her slumber around high noon, Lady Park lashed at her saying, "You, evil girl! Do you think I don't know that you are a spy from Qing China whose name is Gi Hong-Dae? Don't even think about doing something here. Go back to your country at once!"

Learning that her cover was blown and even her dagger was

taken away, Gi Hong-Dae bowed before Lady Park and begged,

"Since my Lady knows everything, what else can I hide? If you spare my life, then I will return to my country and live quietly."

Lady Park sent Gi Hong-Dae away. Though she tried to run away, all four sides of the backyard were surrounded by high cliffs. Gi Hong-Dae kept moving about the backyard and could not find a way out.

Then, Lady Park appeared and said,

"If I had sent you away, I am sure that you would have gone to slay General Im Gyung-Up. So, I displayed a little of my supernatural powers. Now, go and tell your king. Tell him that there are many people like me in Joseon and he should not make light of this country."

As soon as she finished speaking, Lady Park recited a chant. Then, the body of Gi Hong-Dae was lifted into the air and was instantly taken to the palace of Qing China. When Gi Hong-Dae reported what happened to her in Joseon, the emperor and empress of Qing China were shocked and at the same time awed by it.

"Though Joseon is small in size, there are many talented characters there. It will not be easy to attack it. But it is also true that there are many corrupt officials in Joseon and the state of affairs is in chaos. If we find a way to bypass Im Gyung-Up, we can definitely succeed. Who among us will lead in the front in attacking Joseon and force it to surrender?"

To this challenge, the brothers Yong Gol-Dae and Yong Yul-Dae stepped forward and said, "If you give us the army, then we will definitely come back with the news of Joseon's surrender."

Rejoicing greatly, the emperor threw a banquet for the two generals and supplied them with soldiers.

Back in Joseon, Lady Park felt an air of uneasiness and told her husband, "Even after the banishment of the spy Gi Hong-Dae, Qing China has not given up on its ambition to attack Joseon. On December 28 of this year, the Qing forces will attack through the East Gate. You should call General Im Gyung-Up in and have him defend the East Gate."

However, the high ranking officials of the government did not care to listen to the words of a woman.

In the end, the forces of Qing China broke through the East Gate and reached the point of overrunning the royal palace.

Lady Park again told her husband, "Now there is nothing to do. Please take the king and flee to the mountain castle of Namhan. I will try to take care of things here."

Yi Shi-Baek did what his wife said.

Soon, Yong Gol-Dae and Yong Yul-Dae led their forces and began ransacking the city of Hanyang. When they learned that the king of Joseon had fled already, they began chasing his followers. Yong Gol-Dae surrounded the mountain castle of Namhan and began to attack it fiercely. The screams of people and horses turned the castle into chaos.

Not being able to see his people getting butchered, the king concurred and wrote Yong Gol-Dae the document of surrender. Then, Yong Gol-Dae took the queen and the crown prince as his captives and left.

On the other hand, the younger brother of Yong Gol-Dae, Yong Yul-Dae, remained in Hanyang and stole the wealth of its citizens and took many women as captives. However, Lady Park protected her relatives and the subjects of the king from the rampage of the barbarians by taking them into Pihwa-Dang. When Yong Yul-Dae entered the house of Yi Shi-Baek, he saw many people gathered in the small backyard which were filled with plantation and all kinds of interesting flowers. At once, Yong Yul-Dae led several hundreds of his soldiers into Pihwa-Dang. Strangely, those plants and flowers that he saw now looked like several thousand soldiers holding banners and weapons. Baffled, Yong Yul-Dae moved deeper and deeper into the place. Then, a young woman pulling a large sword appeared and screamed at him.

"You, rascal! Aren't you Yong Yul-Dae, a general of barbarians? I am Gye-Hwa, the maidservant of Lady Park, the wife of Sir Yi Shi-Baek. Since you attacked a foreign country and killed many innocent lives, you must pay the price. Here, taste my sword!"

Though he felt lightheaded for a moment, he regained his calmness and replied, "You think you know everything, don't you? You little girl! If I do not capture you and vent my rage, how can I be called a general of Qing China?"

But Yong Yul-Dae was no match for Gye-Hwa. Immediately, Yong Yul-Dae's head was cut off by the blade of Gye-Hwa's sword. All the barbarian soldiers scattered and ran away once they lost their leader. Lady Park hung Yong Yul-Dae's head in a high place so that everyone could see it.

On his way from the mountain castle of Namhan after obtaining the surrender of the king of Joseon, Yong Gol-Dae came upon the place where the head of his younger brother hung. Not being able to control his rage, he tried to rush to Pihwa-Dang where Lady Park was. However, all the trees surrounding Pihwa-Dang turned into soldiers and fought against Yong Gol-Dae. He could not get near Pihwa-Dang. Then, he tried to set Pihwa-Dang on fire. But Lady Park performed her magic and had the wind blow in the opposite direction. The flame instead surrounded the barbarians.

Realizing that he risked his own life by continuing to attack, Yong Gol-Dae decided to retreat his forces. Taking the queen, the crown prince, many women, and all kinds of treasure with him, Yong Gol-Dae tried to return to Qing China. Then, Lady Park instructed Gye-Hwa to relay the following message.

"You ignorant barbarians, if you take our queen away, then I am not going to let anyone of you remain alive. Just return home without anything."

When Yong Gol-Dae refused, Lady Park performed her magic and had the sky pour down snow and rain on the soldiers. The barbarians could not move a step because of the blizzard.

Finally, not being able to withstand Lady Park's magic, Yong Gol-Dae knelt before her and begged for his life.

"Though I have eyes, I do not have eyeballs and I committed a great sin against you, my lady. As you commanded, I will not take the queen with me. Please have mercy on me and spare my life. I will just return to my country and live there quietly."

With a loud voice, Lady Park lashed at him.

"I want to cut off your head and wash the shame of my country away. But since that is not the will of heaven, I will send you away free. From now on, do not belittle Joseon because of its small size. I will never, ever forgive the next time."

After apologizing a hundred times to Lady Park, Yong Gol-Dae retreated back to his country with his soldiers.

It is said that Lady Park and Yi Shi-Baek continued to serve their country faithfully and manage their household affairs wisely until they reached the age of eighty and died together at the same hour of the same day.

Defending the mountain castle of Namhan for forty five days!

The mountain castle of Namhan, along with the mountain castle of Bukhan, was a fortress protecting the capital city of Hanyang. During the Second Manchu Invasion of Korea of 1636, this was also the place where King Injoe personally led the Joseon army and fought against the invading forces of the Qing Dynasty of China for forty five days.

The mountain castle of Namhan had four command posts, one in each of the four corners. The command post was called Jangdae and was the place from which the commander would direct soldiers in battle. Of the four command posts, only one, which was located in the west called Sueo-Jangdae, survived. The sign Sueo-Jangdae is hanging on the front exterior of the building and the sign Mumangru is hanging on the interior of the building. The name Mumangru was given in the memory of King Injoe and his son, King Hyojong. It means that King Injoe's hardships during the Second Manchu Invasion of Korea, along with King Hyojong's failure and death while trying to take the northern territory from the Qing Dynasty to retaliate his father, should never be forgotten.

Sueo-Jangdae

Sahssi Namjeonggi

Lady Sah's Adventures to the South

Lady Sah's Adventures to the South is a novel written by Kim Man-Jung (1637–1692) during the reign of King Sukjong of Joseon. The original title literally means, "The story of a woman with the last name Sah, who traveled to the south." It is a story about Lady Sah's struggles, an honorable and wise woman, who was forced out of her house when an evil mistress took residence in the household.

Within the world of *yangbans* during the Joseon Dynasty, there was a custom that allowed men to keep mistresses besides their lawfully wedded wives. Due to this arrangement, there were many instances where household peace was wrecked due to the conflict between the wife and the mistress. The same practice existed for the kings of Joseon as well. Kings had queens which they assigned the position as the mother of the kingdom to whom they married in royal weddings;

not only did the kings have their queens, but they also had many other women as mistresses. The upper class tried to gain power by marrying their daughters to the king and this added to the conflict between the queen and royal mistresses.

This novel actually ridicules the historical incident in which King Sukjong overthrew and forced Queen In-Hyun out of the palace and installed Lady Jang, his royal mistress, as the new queen. Kim Man-Jung angered the king by speaking against the decision, and as a result was banished from the kingdom.

It is said that Kim Man-Jung wrote this novel while in exile. It seems like he tried to change King Sukjong's heart by it. The main characters in the novel, Yu Yun-Su, Lady Sah and Lady Gyo, represent King Sukjong, Queen In-Hyun, and Lady Jang the royal mistress respectively. Because of the sensitive nature of the subject matter, the author must have worked hard to avoid any direct connection with the king. The historical and spatial context of the novel was set in Suncheon, China.

In the novel, the main character Lady Sah suffers a great deal of hardship but ultimately returns home justified. However, Lady Gyo finds a cruel end, just like the old saying that the honorable and good receive blessings whereas the wicked ultimately become ruined. This proves to be true in the novel *Lady Sah's Adventures to the South*.

During the Ming Dynasty, a boy named Yu Yun-Su lived in the province of Sunchun, China. Yu's grandfather, Yu Gi, was a renowned hero for his contribution to the founding of the dynasty and his father was Yu Hyun. His mother, Lady Choi, died early and it was his father who raised Yu Yun-Su. Fortunately, his father received help from his sister, Lady Du, who lived close by and was there to assist in all the affairs of the household.

At the age of fifteen, Yu Yun-Su, who was handsome in appearance and smart, passed the test to become a government official. When the emperor appointed him to the position of

186

a royal librarian, Yu Yun-Su humbly declined the offer, saying that he was too young and needed to study more. Impressed by Yu's attitude, the emperor gave him special permission to go and study for five more years before returning. Though he was yet to start his government career, people called him "Scholar Yu."

In the meantime, his father Yu Hyun decided to find a mate for his son and get him married. He sought for a suitable candidate in all the places he knew, but he could not find one that pleased him.

One day, a matchmaker gave him advice.

"If you prefer a family that is rich and of high status, then there is no other family better than Minister Uhm. If you seek a woman of wisdom and good character, then there is no one better than Miss Jeong-Ok. She is the daughter of Clerk Sah who lives in the town of Sinseong County."

Yu Hyun also knew Clerk Sah. He was a man of upright character and principles, and, having been falsely charged, was currently in exile in a faraway land. Yu thought a daughter of the family of that level would surely be wise and good. When he consulted with his sister Lady Du, she proposed a clever plan.

She said,

"It says that a person's handwriting reveals much about

his or her character, doesn't it? Since we were about to send a drawing of the Buddha to Temple Wu-Hwa, why don't we ask the Buddhist nun Myo-Hye of the temple to go and get a writing written by Miss Jeong-Ok?"

Accordingly, the Buddhist nun Myo-Hye went over to the house of Clerk Sah, along with a Buddha drawing. Myo-Hye thought that Lady Jeong-Ok's face, which had a fair and dignified look, resembled that of Buddha in the drawing. Then, the monk pulled out the drawing and showed it to her and asked her to write a poem in praise of Buddha.

However, Miss Jeong-Ok refused and said,

"How can I, lacking in literary talents, compose such a piece? Besides, since long ago, people do not like the idea of women composing literary pieces, do they?"

"Composing a poem that praises Buddha is more valuable than giving a great deal of riches in alms. Since this particular Buddha is a female, wouldn't it be fitting to have a poem composed by a woman in her praise?"

Hearing these words from the Buddhist nun Myo-Hye, Jeong-Ok was moved to pick up a writing brush and wrote a line of praise on the bottom of the drawing. The Buddhist nun Myo-Hye saw how beautiful Jeong-Ok's writing was and was amazed once again.

Nervously, Yu Hyun and Lady Du awaited the return of Myo-Hye. After hearing about the beautiful writing by Myo-Hye, they made a decision. At once, Yu Hyun sent word to the household of Clerk Sah expressing his desire to receive Miss Jeong-Ok as his son's wife. Though the family of Clerk Sah declined politely at first, they accepted the marriage proposal when the town magistrate took it upon himself to lay the ground work between the families. In this way, the wedding of Yu Yun-Su and Sah Jeong-Ok came to pass.

The two were a perfect couple. Lady Sah was a wise woman, who respected the elderly and treated her servants graciously. The marital relationship was blissful and the household was always filled with laughter. All the servants respected and followed Lady Sah. Yu Hyun, who had been faithfully cared by Lady Sah for a long time, grabbed his son's hand and said on his deathbed,

"Your wife is truly virtuous and wise. Even in the face of all kinds of hardship, you must live together, trust each other, and consult each other in happiness."

Time passed and it was ten years since they married each

other. Though the marital bliss between Yu Yun-Su and Lady Sah was intact, they did not have a child together. After a great deal of worrying, Lady Sah told her husband,

"Since my body is weak, I cannot seem to bear a child. I consider it a grave sin. If it goes on like this, I am afraid that the ancestry of the Yu Family would come to an end. I think it is wise to bring in an honorable and healthy woman through whom the family ancestry can be continued."

"I cannot have a mistress just because we do not have a child. Besides, there is a possibility that the household can become chaotic when a mistress moves in. Why do you want to risk such a thing? You should not be entertained with such a thought and we should just wait a while."

Despite this reply of Yu Yun-Su, Lady Sah could not sit around and wait for something to happen indefinitely. Through a matchmaker, Lady Sah inquired about a virgin and made a recommendation to her husband once again.

"There is a woman named Chae-Ran with the last name Gyo. They say she is healthy and has the look of being able to give birth to a son."

When nudged by his wife several times, Yu Yun-Su unwillingly brought Lady Gyo in as his second wife. Indeed, Lady Gyo was beautiful like a flower. She conceived immediately and at the end of ten months, she gave birth to a healthy and handsome child.

Yu Yun-Su was greatly pleased and named the child Jang-Ju, and cherished Lady Gyo all the more. Lady Sah also doted on Jang-ju as if he were her own child, and treated Lady Gyo with more kindness.

However, after the birth of the son, Lady Gyo's ambitions began to surface. She desired to push Lady Sah out of the family and become the first wife in her place.

Not long after Lady Gyo gave birth to a son, Lady Sah also became miraculously pregnant. And in ten months, she gave birth to a son who was named In-Ah.

More than ten years passed since Yu Yun-Su got married, so Yu Yun-Su had all but given up on having a son through his first wife. Now, his joy of having another son was greater than at the time of Jang-Ju's birth. He threw a huge banquet and all the family members and acquaintances congratulated him. However, only one person was burning with jealousy and that was Lady Gyo.

Lady Gyo hired a shaman named Ship-Ryang and consulted as to how she could get rid of Lady Sah.

Shaman Ship-Ryang played a trick and had Jang-Ju, the son of Lady Gyo, come down with a sickness. Then, the shaman accused Lady Sah for putting a curse on Jang-Ju. Lady Gyo threw a temper tantrum saying that Lady Sah was trying to kill her son. However, Yu Yun-Su defended Lady Sah saying that a good woman like Lady Sah could never do something like that. This attitude of Yu Yun-Su towards Lady Sah only inflamed Lady Gyo's jealousy all the more.

Meanwhile, the urgent news of the grave illness of her mother reached Lady Sah. Having entrusted the care of the household to Lady Gyo, Lady Sah left for her mother's house hastily. Coincidentally, Scholar Yu was given the royal authorization to go and tour the provinces that were suffering due to a famine and had to leave the house for some time.

There was now a cunning and dishonest caretaker named Dong-Chung in Yu's household. Lady Gyo and Dong-Chung were similar in spirit in that they both had deceitful and ambitious characters. With Yu Yun-Su and Lady Sah out of the house, the two paraded with each other openly, altered the family wealth, and created a plan to push Lady Sah out.

One day while traveling through the land sneakily, Yu Yun-

Su came upon a tavern and met a young man named Naeng-Jin. As the two were chatting about many different things, Yu accidentally saw a jade ring that was hanging on Naeng-Jin's coat string. He realized that the jade ring was the one and only ring that his father gave to his wife Lady Sah as an heirloom. He asked Naeng-Jin about how he got the ring, but with only a mysterious smirk on his face, Naeng-Jin did not say much. Instantly, Yu Yun-Su became confused and began doubting his wife.

After several months, Yu Yun-Su returned home and looked for Lady Sah immediately. Lady Sah, having returned from her mother's funeral, was also home.

"Dear, do you have the jade ring that my father gave you in a safe place?"

"Of course, I kept it in the jewelry box. But how come you are asking about it?"

When the jewelry box was opened, however, the jade ring was missing. Lady Gyo apparently had Lady Sah's maidservant Seol-Mae steal it and give it to a friend of Dong-Chung, Naeng-Jin. Without knowing these things, Yu Yun-Su lashed out at Lady Sah. Lady Sah could only keep her head down and remain silent.

In that moment, Lady Du walked in to the room. Then, Yu Yun-Su told Lady Du about everything from meeting Naeng-Jin in a faraway province to seeing him with the jade ring. Lady Sah was left speechless by what she heard.

Then, Lady Du rebuked Yu Yun-Su saying,

"It is clear that someone in this household tried to frame Lady Sah. Do not be swayed by these things but investigate to disclose the truth."

Yu Yun-Su called his servants in one by one and questioned them. He even ordered them to be beaten. But no one said anything about the jade ring. Seol-Mae thought about what Lady Gyo said; she would kill her if she told the truth. This made Seol-Mae keep her mouth shut.

As the jade ring incident came to an end with no resolution, Yu Yun-Su started to doubt Lady Sah little by little. On top of that, even Lady Du, who acted as protection for Lady Sah, followed her son to a different area. Once Lady Du, whom Lady Sah trusted and relied on like her mother, left, Lady Sah became insecure and lonely. Since Lady Du, who thought ill of Lady Gyo disappeared, Lady Gyo was relieved.

Lady Gyo, sharing affections with Dong-Chung, made a frightful plan. It was a plan to kick Lady Sah out once and for all.

Jang-Ju, Lady Gyo's son, had been declining in health ever since becoming ill due to Ship-Ryang's trick several years before. It did not seem like he was ever going to get better. He kept getting weaker despite all the medicine he took. Then, one day, Jang-Ju threw up blood and died instantly after taking the medicine prepared by Chun-Bang, a servant of Lady Sah. Lady Gyo was shocked and cried hysterically. Upon hearing the commotion, Yu came running.

"Someone poisoned the medicine Jang-Ju took."

Hearing these words, Yu fed what remained of the medicine to the dog. The dog died on the spot.

"This is surely the work of Lady Sah!"

Of course, the murder of Jang-Ju was set up by Lady Gyo, Dong-Chung, and Ship-Ryang. In order to get rid of Lady Sah, Lady Gyo went as far as killing her own son. Yu Yun-Su who was clueless about the truth became enraged and ended up banishing Lady Sah from the house. Lady Sah had to leave her crying baby behind and was forced into the palanquin like a prisoner. Seeing Lady Sah like this, many relatives and servants turned around to wipe their tears.

After being banished, rather than returning to the house of her parents, Lady Sah built a temporary cottage next to the grave of her father-in-law, who used to cherish her, and lived there. Though Lady Gyo kept pressuring Yu Yun-Su to send her away from the grave and to a faraway place, Yu could not bring himself to do it. Lady Gyo, out of anger, decided to have Naeng-Jin kidnap Lady Sah.

Then, Lady Gyo imitated the handwriting of Lady Du and forged a letter. The message was that it was dangerous for Lady Sah to live alone lest something bad happened to her, and Lady Sah should come and stay with her. Lady Sah thought the letter really came from Lady Du and wrote her back saying that she would do as advised and needed a palanquin to travel in.

However, her deceased father-in-law, Yu Hyun, appeared to her in a dream that night.

"The letter you received was not from Lady Du and you should not follow its instruction. For the next seven years, a lot of bad things will happen to you. Flee to the south and persevere through the difficult time. Six years from now, on April 15, you should dock a boat in the water and rescue a certain person who is on the run. Then, from that point on, your life would change for the better. Keep these words in mind."

When she woke up from the dream, Lady Sah turned away from Naeng-Jin's people who brought her the palanquin. Then, she boarded a ship that was going to the south along with three servants.

As they traveled in the ship toward the south, they came upon a squall and almost died. Those on board the ship suffered seasickness and collapsed one by one. The crew docked the ship in shallow water and searched for people on the land to ask for help. Lady Sah and her servants came upon a nice young woman. She allowed them to stay at her house. The woman's name was Chwee-Young, and she cared for Lady Sah earnestly. Within a few days, Lady Sah and Chwee-Young became like sisters. When she recovered from her sickness, Lady Sah had to be on her way again. The two women found it hard to part their ways. Lady Sah took the ring off her finger and gave it to Chwee-Young as a sign of her affection.

Now, Lady Sah boarded the ship again and set sail. This time, the servant who had been faithful became sick with a local illness and eventually died.

She ran out of money and there was no one she knew. Now,

with the death of her faithful servant, Lady Sah became weak in spirit. Her body and mind were exhausted and only the thought of throwing herself into the river remained.

Lady Sah stripped the bark off a pine tree that stood on a nearby hill and wrote the following words.

> *"On this certain day of this certain month, Jeong-Ok shed her tears and threw herself into the river."*

As Lady Sah was about to jump into the river, a certain Buddhist nun came to her and bowed to her with her hands put together. Upon close inspection, Lady Sah realized that it was the Buddhist nun Myo-Hye who once came to visit her. Apparently, the nun had received a revelation from Buddha and came to rescue Lady Sah. After that day, Lady Sah stayed with Myo-Hye in a small cottage named Temple Su-Wol.

In the meantime, having gotten rid of Lady Sah, Lady Gyo took residence in the main chamber of the house and carried on pretentiously as if the world was hers. Whenever Yu Yun-Su was out of the house, Lady Gyo and Dong-Chung acted like a couple and pushed the servants around. Because Lady Gyo liked to dispense beatings and harsh punishments capriciously, all the servants missed the gracious Lady Sah.

"Now, all the wealth will be ours if only Yu Yun-Su disappears."

Then, the two conspired to kill Yu Yun-Su and take over the wealth.

One day, Dong-Chung came upon something that Yu Yun-Su had written and slapped his knees in excitement.

At once, Dong-Chung ran to Minister Uhm and showed him the writing of Yu Yun-Su. It pointed out the incompetency of the emperor. Uhm, who did not like Yu Yun-Su to begin with, presented the writing to the emperor immediately. The emperor was enraged and sent Yu Yun-Su into exile.

With Yu Yun-Su in exile, Dong-Chung earned the trust of Minister Uhm and was given the position of a provincial official. Lady Gyo packed all the jewels in the house and went on the road with Dong-Chung.

Fearing that In-Ah, the son of Lady Sah, might take revenge on her when grown up, Lady Gyo ordered the maidservant Seol-Mae to kill the child. However, Seol-Mae could not bring herself to kill In-Ah, who was asleep. Instead, she abandoned the child who was wrapped in a quilt in the woods. Then, she lied to Lady Gyo that she threw the child into the water.

Several years later, there was a royal banquet to celebrate the anointing of the crown prince by the emperor. For this reason, Yu Yun-Su was freed from his exile and able to return home at last.

When he was passing through a certain town, he came upon the associates of a provincial official. He was surprised to see the arrogant official seated on the top of the white horse. It was no other than Dong-Chung who used to be the foreman in his house. Yu Yun-Su was mystified at how Dong-Chung was able to rise to such a high position.

All his questions were answered at once when he met Seol-Mae. Following the associates from behind, she spotted Yu Yun-Su and ran to him at once.

She began crying and confessed.

"Lady Sah had been gracious to me, but I did not realize that and I did wrong. For a long time, Lady Gyo and Dong-Chung devised an evil plan without anyone knowing. Being a fool, I was tricked by Lady Gyo. I stole the jade ring that belongs to Lady Sah and even put poison in Jang-Ju's medicine. Lady Sah was framed with the wrongdoing and was kicked out mainly because of what I did."

Hearing these words, Yu Yun-Su could only lament. "Because

I was foolish, I was deceived by evil Lady Gyo. Now, I cannot face my ancestors!"

Seol-Mae even divulged that she was ordered to kill In-Ah.

"Lady Gyo ordered me to drown In-Ah, but I could not bring myself to do it. I left In-Ah in the woods and someone nice might have rescued him. At times, I prayed to the gods in heaven that he was saved.

"If In-Ah is alive, then he owes his life to you."

It was reported to Lady Gyo that Seol-Mae met Scholar Yu, and Seol-Mae died by hanging herself.

After parting ways with Seol-Mae, Yu Yun-Su wandered around the river bank in deep sadness. By chance, he came upon the words that were written on the bark of a pine tree.

"On this certain day of this certain month, Jeong-Ok shed her tears and threw herself into the river."

Yu Yun-Su realized that these were Lady Sah's words and began wailing.

"My innocent wife died because of me! How can I pay for this sin! I must comfort her spirit by offering a memorial ceremony."

202

As he was shedding tears and writing down the words of tribute, he heard a strange sound. When he looked outside, he saw tens of tough-looking men surrounding his residence. Dong-Chung had sent his servants to kill him. Yu Yun-Su barely escaped and found himself at the river bank one more time. When he could not go any further, he decided to die.

"I am receiving the punishment for mistreating my good wife. Rather than dying at my enemy's hands, I should throw myself into the river."

In that moment, a boat slowly moved in front of Yu Yun-Su. The person moving the oars was a Buddhist nun. As soon as the boat reached the riverbank, Yu Yun-Su jumped over onto the boat. The boat then moved out to the middle of the river with Yu Yun-Su on board. The mob of Dong-Chung's servants cried, "The murderer is running away," and signalled the boat to turn around right away. However, the female monk acted as if she did not hear them and continued to push her oars away. Yu Yun-Su began explaining his situation to the nun.

"I am a royal archivist and my name is Yu Yun-Su. Do not believe their words that I am a murderer. They are just making this up."

A woman who was sitting in the corner of the boat suddenly

lifted her head upon hearing these words of Yu. Yu then took a close look at her face and realized it was his wife, Lady Sah.

"My dear husband!"

"My wife!"

Lady Sah had remembered what her father-in-law instructed her in her dream many years ago. When it became April 15, she came out to the river with Myo-Hye. It was her one and only husband whom she saved.

The couple embraced each other and cried for some time. They also told each other what happened during their time of separation.

Yu Yun-Su disclosed, among many things, that it was the wickedness of Lady Gyo that had Lady Sah framed, that Dong-Chung caused him to be exiled, and that Lady Gyo plundered the wealth of the family and ran away with Dong-Chung. Though Lady Sah was able to hear about all these things in silence, when she heard that In-Ah was abandoned and it was not clear whether he survived or not, she fainted.

Yu Yun-Su looked after Lady Sah earnestly. Due to his faithful caring, Lady Sah was able to emerge from her grief of losing In-Ah.

As Yu Yun-Su was leaving Temple Su-Wol, he promised Lady Sah, "I will go first and take care of the household. I will also go and look after my ancestors' graves. Then, I will come back and take you with me properly."

Away from the sight of Dong-Chung's thugs, Yu Yun-Su traveled to his hometown, Sunchun. There, he minded his remaining wealth and estate and managed the hill where his ancestors were buried.

One day, a servant who returned from reporting the harvest to Lady Sah, informed Yu Yun-Su,

"In the town court of Yakju, there is a notice posted in search for you. The emperor has bestowed on you the high position of government and is waiting for you to report."

While Yu was living in seclusion in his hometown, many things happened in the royal court. Minister Uhm was exposed of immense corruption and was sent into exile after having been stripped of his position and wealth. Dong-Chung, who accumulated great wealth through many heinous acts of wickedness, was also arrested and executed. The emperor, after getting rid of all of Minister Uhm's cohorts, recalled all loyal officials that had formerly been either exiled or demoted.

Upon finding out about this development, Yu Yun-Su left right away. He then went to the palace and met with the emperor.

The emperor called Yu to his side and grabbed his hand. Then, he apologized to Yu for his failure to previously recognize Yu's loyalty.

When Yu Yun-Su returned to his old house as a high-ranking official, all the servants came out to greet him and cried tears of joy. Lady Du, who had previously moved to the countryside with her son was also back in the house and greeted him.

Finally, when the preparation was finished, Yu Yun-Su brought Lady Sah back. The couple went to bow before the graves of their ancestors and were reunited as husband and wife. Lady Sah arranged the funeral for her servant who died while faithfully caring for her. Moreover, she sent many gifts to Myo-Hye to thank her for all the help she received.

Now, everything was back in its place except for her son, In-Ah, who could not be found. Worrying that the lineage of her family would be cut off, Lady Sah called Chwee-Young, who once cared for her dearly when she was on the run. Lady Sah was surprised to find out that Chwee-Young was Myo-Hye's niece.

Lady Sah held Chwee-Young's hand and requested her in earnest to become the second wife of her husband. Remembering the words of Myo-Hye that she would become the wife of a minister, Chee-Young accepted the proposal in gratitude.

Chwee-Young had an adopted brother. He was found crying outside her house. Her family took him in and raised him. After the deaths of her parents, she had been taking care of him.

One day, the former nanny for In-Ah came to visit Chwee-Young.

"I heard that your brother looked a lot like In-Ah, the one I used to take care of. Can I take a look at him?"

As soon as the child stepped inside the room, the nanny recognized that he was In-Ah. The boy also recognized the nanny. The nanny hugged the child and ran to Lady Sah.

Lady Sah and Yu Yun-Su could not believe that In-Ah was back and alive.

"Is this a dream or is this real? If it is a dream, please do not wake me!"

After this, Lady Sah cherished Chwee-Young all the more, and Chwee-Young respected Lady Sah as her senior.

On the other hand, what had happened to Lady Gyo?

After Dong-Chung's death, she ran away with Naeng-Jin. But immediately, she was robbed clean by robbers and became dirt poor. When even Naeng-Jin was accused of being a traitor and was executed, she became a mistress at a tavern. While working at the tavern, she boasted to others that she had once been the wife of a royal archivist.

Upon hearing about Lady Gyo, Yu Yun-Su and Lady Sah sent people to bring her in. When Lady Gyo dismounted from the palanquin, she realized that it was none other than the house of Yu Yun-Su and her face turned red in fear.

"Please, I beg you, spare me. It was Seol-Mae who killed Jang-Ju and stole the jade ring."

Lady Gyo tried to save herself by blaming Seol-Mae who was already died for her sins.

This infuriated Yu Yun-Su all the more and immediately ordered her to be executed. Lady Gyo fought hysterically until her last breath. After learning that her maidservant, Seol-Mae, died unfairly, Lady Sah collected her bones and buried them properly.

Having overcome all kinds of hardship, Yu Yun-Su and Lady Sah lived long into their eighties and enjoyed many blessings of life. Lady Sah wrote books to teach her descendants. The second wife, Chwee-Young, had three sons and they all reached high positions in the royal court. Chwee-Young and Lady Sah treated each other with utmost respect and lived happily ever after.

Was Lady Jang really an evil woman?

Lady Jang was the royal mistress of King Sukjong, the nineteenth king of Joseon. She used to be nothing more than a palace woman before being loved by the king. She reached the highest status among the royal mistresses and even became the queen for a while when the original queen, Queen In-Hyun, was dethroned.

She came to be known as the most evil woman of Joseon. She was notorious for being intensely jealous and ambitious as shown in her action of harassing and kicking Queen In-Hyun out of the palace. Come to think of it, however, both women were the sacrificial lambs in a political game and we should look at both of them with pity.

During the time of King Sukjong's reign, the royal court was divided into two camps and there was great conflict between the two. The politicians were divided into the camp of westerners supporting Queen In-Hyun and the camp of southerners supporting Lady Jang. They engaged in campaigns of mudslinging and slandering against each other. The camp of southerners that used to be weaker, used Lady Jang's influence to expand their power. When Lady Jang stole the heart of King Sukjong and bore him a son, who was later made prince, there was commotion among the westerners. Now, there was a backfire of opinion in the court that a son of a royal mistress could never be made a prince. King Sukjong thought that the disagreeing view was the work of the queen and forced the queen out of the palace. Then, the king sent all the influential figures among the westerners into exile. Kim Man-Jung, the author of *Lady Sah's Adventures to the South*, was a westerner and was separated to the region of Namhae of South Gyeongsang Province. While he was there, he wrote the novel.

After a while, the political climate changed again and Queen In-Hyun was restored to her place and Lady Jang was relegated to a low status. However, unlike Lady Sah in the novel, Queen In-Hyun did not get to spend the last years of her life in peace. By the time she returned to the palace, she had already been sick for some time and did not live much longer. Also, Lady Jang was charged with the crime of placing a curse on Queen In-Hyun. In the end, Lady Jang reaches death by drinking poison.

Gyujung Chilwu Jaengronggi

The Story of Seven Friends
in a Woman's Quarters

The Story of Seven Friends in a Woman's Quarters tells the story of seven tools used in sewing: a needle, a thread, a ruler, a heart-shaped iron, a flat iron, a thimble, and a pair of scissors. It is an entertaining tale of how each of these tools claims that they should be given more credit, until the woman in the women's quarter rebukes them. The story brings to life sewing tools to parody human's way of living.

The women of a *yangban* birthright during the Joseon era lived a life disconnected from the outside world, due to the influence of Confucianism. From a room located in the intimate corner of the house, they would learn how to sew until their parents selected a man for them to marry. From then on, their life would mostly require serving their husband, bearing children, and raising them well. It would not be an exaggeration to say their sewing tools were their closest friends, since they spent most of their time in privacy.

For some women, writing was their only escape from their mundane life. This story is also said to have been written by an unknown woman during the Joseon era. Judging from how she is able to bring out the unique qualities of each of the sewing tools in the woman's quarters and illustrates them as if they were human, the writer must have been a very observant woman.

Inside a woman's quarters, there reside seven friends, the only friends the woman may have had.

The ladies working in the house, also kept their sewing tools close, naming them and befriending them. The needle was called the *seyo* which means 'thin waist' bride, the ruler was called the *cheok* Chinese for *ja* lady, the scissors was the *gyodu* interwined heads bride, and the heart-shaped iron was called the *inhwa* attracting fire lady. The flat iron was called the *wul* maiden, the thread was the *cheonghongheukbaek* which refers to the colors blue, red, black, white bride, and the thimble was the old *gamtu* lady.

When the lady of the house washes up, puts on makeup and heads out for the day, the seven friends gather, discuss the work they need to complete for the day, and begin the tasks assigned to them.

One day, while sewing, the seven friends each began to boast of their merits.

Showing off her long waist, the *cheok* lady [the ruler] said,

"Hey, listen to what I have to say. When we're cutting cloths like thin silk, thick silk, white ramie, and hemp cloths, you guys need me to properly measure the long, the short, the wide, and the narrow. How else will you make clothes? So, *I* contribute the most when it comes to making clothes."

Then, the *gyodu* bride [the scissors] came forward, and quickly manipulating her two legs, said,

"*Cheok* lady, no matter how well you measure out the clothes, it wouldn't come out looking half as good unless I cut them well. Without my merits and efforts, nothing would amount to anything. So, don't go on boasting."

The *seyo* bride [the needle], bending her thin waist, rebuked both of them and said,

"Both of you are wrong. You may have ten bowls of pearls, but you have to sew them together to make them into beads. You guys can measure out the fabrics, cut them, and iron them all you want, but without me, you simply can't make clothes. Thread them fine, thread them thick, thread the short sleeves or thread the long ones—without my quick and speedy skills, you can't get the fabrics to look the way you want them to."

Then, the *cheonghongheukbaek* bride *the thread*, with her face red, became upset and cried,

"*Seyo*—technically speaking, your accomplishments are my accomplishments. You can pretend to be nice and skilful all you want, but without me, you're nothing."

At that remark, the old *gamtu* lady *the thimble* chuckled and said,

"My dear brides. Will you please stop boasting?

Am I not helping our dear lady and making sure she does not hurt her little fingers? There's an old saying—"You are better off being the head of a chicken than the tale of a cow. *In other words, it is better to be the head of a mediocre institution than follow the shadow of a brilliant person.*

Cheonghong bride, you're doing nothing but following *seyo* bride around—so why do you keep on boasting so? You do great damage to that pretty face of yours. I may be pierced by the ears of *seyo* all the time, but my leathers are thick and the

piercings are bearable. I won't say anymore."

Then, the *inhwa* lady ^{heart-shaped iron} said, "Girls, please stop arguing and listen to what I have to say. Who could make the sewing on the quilt as fine as chopsticks, and the sewing on the seam like it's been glued? The sewing could be done badly, but as soon as I touch it with my pretty little fingers, the mistake disappears like a shadow. *I* deserve all the praise."

At that, the *wul* maiden ^{the flat iron} opened her mouth wide, and chuckled out loud.

"*Inhwa*, your task and mine are the same. But *inhwa*, you may only iron the part of the clothing where there's been sewing done, but I iron all types of clothes everywhere. Even the most wrinkled clothes become nice and straight once my wide buttocks pass by it. And what's more, when summer time comes, I have so much work to do that I can't even get a glimpse of rest during the day. Without me, how would you straighten out the clothes that have been twisted  and dried. How

could the people of the world wear wrinkled clothes?
So it's settled; it's me who should receive all the praise."

Then the lady of the house, who had only been listening to their conversation, stepped up and said,

"Everyone, be quiet. I require all seven of your help in making clothes, but the merits differ depending on the person in charge of the tools. Then how can all of you claim that you deserve all the praise?"

With that said, the lady pushed all seven of her friends aside, and, placing her pillow at her head, went to sleep.

The *cheok* lady the ruler sighed and began,

"How cruel humans are, and especially ignorant are women! Does the lady not look for me first and foremost when she is making clothes, and only claim that *she* has done it all after she's done using me? When she's waking up that wretched servant girl of hers, she always uses *me*. She doesn't even care that she can break my back like that. How could she be so cold hearted? I am so angry that I can't stand it.

The *gyodu* bride the scissors continued to say,

"You're right. She can't cut the fabric without me, but often, she

218

complains that I don't work well and throws me around. She sometimes takes my two legs and shakes them really hard. I'm just sickened when she does that. When the *seyo* bride runs away to take a break, the lady acts like it is all my fault. It's not like I've hidden her. But she hangs me upside down on the door hook and turns me this way and that until she finds her. I can't tell you how many times she has done that to me. But she doesn't even acknowledge what I've done for her? I'm just sad and miserable."

The *seyo* bride ^{the needle} also sighed and said,

"That's nothing compared to what I've had to endure. Why do I have to be pestered and abused by human hands? Do you know how hard I work to help with the sewing, even with my weak back and tip? Do you know how many times she's broken me and thrown me on the charcoal burner? Would you not be frustrated if you were me? Sometimes I poke under her nails and get her to bleed–that gets me feeling a lot better. But I can't even do that well when the old *gamtu* lady is in the way. All of this is really hard on me, let me tell you."

The *inhwa* lady ^{the heart-shaped iron} shed tears as she said,

"You girls call *that* painful? For what great sin I have to be heated and burned, I'll never know. Every time something hard needs to be broken, she burns my face with the fire from the charcoal burner. I can't even begin to describe how sorrowful and miserable that makes me."

The *wul* maiden ^{the flat iron} also with a depressed look, said,

"*Inhwa*, it looks like we do the same work and get the same bad treatment. I don't know why she has to hold my neck tight and press me down on her clothes. I feel suffocated. My body and my mind get so hazy that I don't know how many times I felt like my neck had a mind of its own."

When the seven friends were complaining about this and that, the lady, who had been sleeping, got up suddenly and screamed, "Why, you have been badmouthing me," with her face darkened with unpleasantness.

Then, the old *gamtu* lady ^{the thimble} stepped up, and with her head bowed low, said,

"These girls are young. They are not   insightful and can't be satisfied. They have their   own sins to deal with, but they have only boasted   of their merits and spoken of their dissatisfactions.

They should rightly be flogged.

But please, think of the love you've begun to have for them and the small merits they *do* deserve. Please forgive them."

After thinking to herself for a little while, the lady nodded.

"All right, I will listen to the old thimble here and will not punish you. The fact that the ends of my fingers are fine is because of her. I will take her with me in a golden pocket, and will not forget the mercy she's displayed upon me. I will have her on me at all times."

The old thimble bowed her head in gratitude and the other friends, in their embarrassment, could not even bear to lift their heads up.

"The four friends of the study"

If the term *gyu-jung-chil-woo* means "the seven friends in a woman's quarters," then the term *mun-bang-sa-woo* means "the four friends in a study where men reside."

Mun-bang was a place where old scholars could work and study. *Seonbis* spent their time with their colleagues in this place, reciting poetry and carrying on discussions. There was no other place that expressed the personality of scholars better than the study. The study required four things: paper, writing brush, ink stick, and ink stone. For this, these four things were called "the four friends of the study," namely *mun-bang-sa-woo*.

Paper was invented in China around 105 A.D. and introduced in Korea around the third or fourth century. A writing brush was made of animal fur such as rabbit fur or weasel fur. The stem of a writing brush was made mainly of bamboo. Initially, burnt pinewood was used to make ink sticks, but now, the ink sticks are made of diesel or lamp oil. Ink is made by pressing and rubbing the ink stick on the ink stone with some water in it. Once the grinded ink gathers in the hollow part of the ink stone, one can dip the tip of the brush in the ink and use it to write on the paper.

The four friends of the study

Writing Brush

Ink stick

Paper

Ink stone